19627
£40

WITHDRAWN FROM STOCK

Kate Malone
A Book of Pots

Lesley Jackson &
Kate Malone

A&C Black London

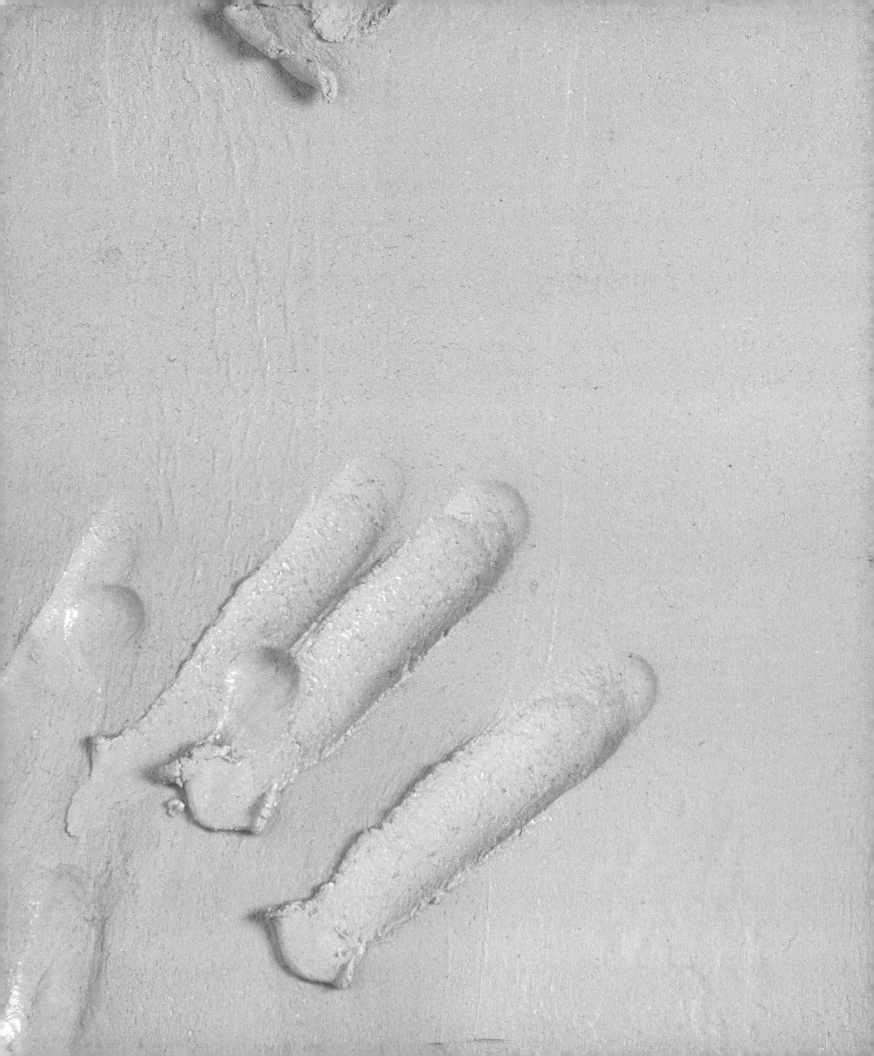

Kate Malone
A Book of Pots

For Mum and Dad, Scarlet and Graham
and the inspiring Dr Deb Doniach

First published in Great Britain 2003
A & C Black Publishers
37 Soho Square
London W1D 3QZ

www.acblack.com

ISBN 0-7136-6180-1

Copyright © Kate Malone & Lesley Jackson 2003

A CIP catalogue record for this book is available from the British Library

Photographs from the Kate Malone Archive.

Design by Katy Hepburn

Printed and bound in Singapore by
Tien Wah Press Pte. Ltd.

Contents

In 1982 I arranged a photo session of my degree show — swapping a piece of work for the photos being taken. I complained that the session was taking ages — the photographer replied that one day these photos would be in a book and that I would not complain then. Twenty years on, dozens of photo sessions later, to my delight, here we are.

I am so excited about this book, it gives me the opportunity to show the full range of my work, to share my techniques and glaze recipes and to illustrate many pieces that have found homes in private collections without having been exhibited in the UK.

I love clay. I am fascinated with the transformation from soft 'stiff' into hard fired ceramic, of powdery poisonous raw glaze into shiny glassy glazes. The sensitivity and versatility of clay is brilliant.

I am inspired by the magic of growth, by nature, by my gurus, by my lovely daughter Scarlet, by living in a vibrant city and doing loads of travelling.

This book covers four areas in which I work. I make short-run production pieces which are like playful sketches and colour trials; I make more 'serious' 'one-of-a-kind' pieces. I make large scale works for the public and private sectors (hospitals and parks, hotels + restaurants), and last but not least I research ceramic glazes, the results of which feeds all the areas of my work.

None of this would have been possible without my ever present and supportive partner Graham — to whom I dedicate this book. I would also like to thank a crowd of family and friends, teachers and collectors. Also my lovely students and very dedicated assistants (past + present). Must not forget also the brilliant photographers, dynamic art dealer, responsive co-writer, caring book designer and encouraging publisher.

Kate Malone.

(hooray for clay).

The Ceramics of Kate Malone
Lesley Jackson

Flying Tigers, 1981-2
h.17cm, l.46cm
Earthenware.
Press-moulded. Coloured
underglazes, clear glaze.
These pieces were made at
Bristol Polytechnic, where
Kate was taught by

luminaries such as Mo Jupp,
Wally Keeler and Nick
Homoky. At the time Kate's
mother bred Siamese cats,
and they provided the
inspiration for these cartoon-
like cat-tigers, created for a
project about camouflage.

The Coles' Family Table,
1985, 240cm x 180cm
Earthenware. Red clay,
white slip, coloured
underglazes, clear and
coloured glazes.
In this transitional piece,
made as a commission
during her second year at
the RCA, Kate looks back to

the tiger imagery developed
at Bristol, and forward to
the marine imagery she
would explore over the
coming years. An ambitious
early attempt at a large-scale
piece fired in a small kiln,
it was created in sections,
fitted together like a giant
jigsaw puzzle.

Flicking through the glorious illustrations in this book, and scrolling through the impressive catalogue of public commissions, a casual observer might conclude that success has come easily to Kate Malone. Since graduating from the Royal College of Art in 1986, she seems to have had one lucky break after another, and from the outset she exuded confidence, optimism and drive. However, the truth of the matter is that it did not just happen. Kate did not hop on the back of a truck and hitch a lift. She designed the juggernaut-jalopy on which she rides, and put herself firmly in the driving seat.

Kate recalls that when she took up her place on a three-year MA at the Royal College of Art, Professor David Hamilton challenged the potential complacency of the new recruits by presenting them with an ultimatum. Either they could carry on where they had left off as undergraduates, and continue making things in the same vein; or they could stretch themselves by tackling new areas and conquering new terrain. Kate was goaded into action. Throwing herself with gusto into a series of design-based course projects, she rose to the challenge of broadening and deepening her understanding of design. This learning developed skills that were later put to use on her large-scale commissions. During her last eighteen months at college she returned to ceramics with renewed vigour, boldly experimenting with new methods of modelling and glazing, pushing the boat out both technically and creatively. Leaving behind the safety of the cuddly tiger-cat formula she had originally hit upon at Bristol Polytechnic, she began to explore a richer vein of imagery inspired by the sea, abandoning flat painting for vivid relief decoration, and replacing flat underglaze colours with deeper, richer watery glaze effects. The key to the success of what eventually emerged as her Fruits of the Sea was not the subject matter per se, but the marriage between imagination and realisation, mind and fingers. It is all very well having ideas, but unless you can bring them alive and arouse curiosity in others, your work will merely please, not compel. By the time of her degree show, Kate had made the leap from amiable to arresting. (See page 10.)

It was her discovery of new techniques of handling and manipulating clay – releasing its potential as a plastic, sculptural medium – that freed her to move forward creatively. Kate has since evolved into a virtuoso modeller – the equivalent of a maestro in the glassmaking world – relishing feats that most potters would shrink from, and (perhaps more remarkably still) firing them successfully. Looking back on her Fruits of the Sea now with the benefit of hindsight, there is more than a hint of youthful bravado about these pieces, particularly gravity-defying creations such as Deep Sea Candelabrum and Fruit Dish (see page 29). In her commentary she speaks of 'whipping up' the clay, but there is also an element of showmanship and whipping up the crowd. The American glass artist Dale Chihuly, the supreme master of spectacle, comes to mind. However, the difference between Malone and Chihuly is that, whereas he keeps pushing his work to ever greater extremes in terms of colour, size and complexity, Kate – having broken the ceramic-sound barrier at a precociously early age – has felt confident enough in her abilities to step back from aerial acrobatic displays. Since the development of her Fruits of the Earth series, she has applied her formidable dexterity to objects which, while not exactly quiet, and certainly not timid, are much more subtle and understated in expression.

Kate's skills are by no means purely manual, however; they extend far beyond the construction of remarkable vessels and the modelling of complex relief decoration. Her pots, whilst undeniably impressive in their raw biscuit-fired state, stand naked without their glazes. Glazes form a crucial part of Kate's artistic repertoire – much more than the proverbial icing on the cake – and her accomplishment in this area should not be underestimated. Over the last fifteen years she has experimented with three distinct families of glazes, starting with multi-coloured, multiple-fired earthenware glazes during the mid 1980s, then branching out in two divergent directions during the early 1990s, exploring low-fired pebble glazes and high-fired crystalline effects. Her interest in glazes began in earnest at the RCA, where she embarked on an ambitious programme of earthenware glaze trials. Literally hundreds of tests were made, with real pots used as vehicles for elaborate multi-layered glaze experiments. Very few potters have worked in this way, and from a technical point of view it is perhaps more apposite to compare Kate's approach to glazes to an artist's handling of paint. Van Gogh's liberal applications of oil paint and liberating colour combinations, for example, are in some ways analogous to Kate's liberated use of glaze. 'Enough! or Too much,' proclaimed William Blake in his Proverbs of Hell, inciting artists to ignore conventional boundaries. Right from the start Kate deliberately overstepped the mark, not out of vanity or foolishness, but through a compulsion to experiment. Some pots were fired fifteen or twenty times over. Even now she regularly combines up to ten glaze firings on a single piece.

Multi-dimensional is perhaps the best way of summarising Kate's pots – physically, aesthetically and psychologically, they operate on several levels. The relationship between the interior and the exterior of the vessel has been a recurrent theme in her work over many years, an awareness that developed after she began to run sprigged motifs over the crest of rims and down inside the neck. Discovering the multi-faceted character of Kate's pots often literally involves a game of hide and seek, with motifs or inscriptions hidden on the sides, and perhaps a rich pool of crystals in the well.

The idea of a vessel within a vessel interests her, an idea first explored in Mrs Deep Sea Meteor (see page 34), whose inner womb is viewed through 'port-holes' in her outer flesh. The double-walled Sliced Fruits represent the culmination of this trend, each piece created as an inner core, then flipped over and sealed with a seamless outer skin.

However, although Kate's Fruits of the Earth have eye-catching forms and ravishing glazes, even at their most extrovert, the detailing is delicate and highly sophisticated. The scrolling harlequin segments on her pineapples, for example, and the curved belly button bases on her gourds, reflect years of subtle refinement. While the physical skill

Royal College of Art MA Degree Show, 1986.
Ever since childhood Kate had been fascinated by the sea, a theme she explored at the RCA through a series of elaborately modelled, hand-built earthenware vessels, mirror frames and candelabra. 'It was here that I realised the true plasticity of wet clay.' Multiple layers of coloured earthenware glazes were the fruits of an ambitious programme of glaze testing.

and technical know-how embodied in her ceramics are apparent at a glance, it is only through examining the pots themselves at close quarters in greater detail that her sensitivity of touch can be fully appreciated. The vital ingredient in the Malone cocktail is the interplay between body and glaze. Although apparently casual, the movement of glazes on the vessel during the firing is in fact carefully planned and controlled. Glazes are applied in specific combinations, in a particular thickness and in a certain order to ensure that they behave in a particular way, while physical details such as roll tops, cupped areas or invisible lips dictate whether they pool or spill. The apparent brashness of Kate's pots is only skin deep. They always repay closer scrutiny.

When she embarked on her Fruits of the Earth, Kate entered a new dimension in terms of psychological complexity. In the last of her Fruits of the Sea she had begun to explore some of the darker and more sinister aspects of marine life and the forces of the deep – the dangers as well as the delights. Although fruit and vegetables might, at first glance, seem a more passive subject than sea creatures, for Kate they have become a potent vehicle for expressing her intense feelings about human relationships and human beings. Without becoming literally humanoid, her pumpkins, pineapples and gourds have frequently taken on distinctive male or female attributes, suggesting the swell of a hip or cleavage, for instance, or the adoption of a specific pose. The birth of her daughter Scarlet in March 1997 stimulated another potent theme: the love of a mother for her child. An outpouring of heart shapes was the most obvious manifestation of this, but there have also been mother-and-daughter pots, emotionally charged, although never cute. (See Mother and Daughter, Pots of Symbols, pages 158-61).

'I'm a doer, not a thinker,' says Kate. 'I work instinctively; I don't intellectualise.' However, this is not to imply that her work is lacking in meaning. It is just that her thought processes operate mainly on a subconscious level, so that she is not always aware of what is driving her. The titles of pots are conceived after the pieces are completed, for example, by a process of post-rationalisation. Always apposite, and often amusing, these titles are invariably illuminating. Over the years Kate has gradually evolved a potent vocabulary of symbols which form the emotional backbone of her work. Jugs for sharing, pineapples for hospitality and prosperity, pumpkins for fertility, and gourds for fecundity. Partly personal, partly universal, these symbols were first embodied in vessel form, but have since been condensed into decorative motifs such as badges, emblems or medals and applied to other pots, acting as shorthand for her philosophy of life.

The seductiveness and accessibility of her themes, combined with the direct visual, tactile and sensuous appeal of the pots themselves, have been key features in the public acceptance of her work. Appealing to both specialists and non-specialists alike, her pots are rare in attracting the attention of connoisseurs of both historical and contemporary ceramics. Her celebrated exhibition *The Allotment*, organised by Midlands Art Centre, which toured ten venues in Britain from 1998-2000, reached

Celery jars made by
James Sadler and other
Staffordshire firms, part of
Kate's extensive collection.

sectors of the public that most potters can only dream of. Her autumn 2002 show at the Geffrye Museum, London, composed of ceramic furniture and furnishings for a complete room setting ('under construction' at the time of writing, see pp. 162-5), has all the makings of a popular classic. Ironically, though, in the concept-orientated contemporary art world, where esotericism and wilful obscurity reign, an artist-potter whose work elicits spontaneous public interest and accolades is regarded with some anxiety and suspicion. Popularity is mistaken for superficiality, and representation for literalism. Kate is a self-confessed addict of fancy dress, whereas many in the art world favour the Emperor's new clothes.

Kate's work constantly challenges the boundaries between high and low culture, so it comes as no surprise to learn that the pots she herself collects are the cheap and cheerful slip-cast celery jars mass-produced by Sadler and various other Staffordshire firms during the post-war period – the kitchen equivalent of garden gnomes. Over the years she has amassed over a hundred of these jars, which meld expressive, quirky human features with relief-moulded foliage and stems. 'I love their seaside postcard madness and their lunatic faces. It's a bit like Arcimboldo or the Green Man – making a pot into a human being.' Other representational characters in the series include lidded pots for pickled onions, beetroot and apple sauce, each coated in an appropriately coloured glaze. 'From a technical point of view I admire the flow of the modelling, and the way the glaze pools in the grooves, enhancing the details of the moulded form.' However, it is the human aspect of these pieces and their zany sense of humour that clearly most appeal to her. Although she does not operate in such a literal or throwaway manner herself, a hint of the slightly demented character of these anthropomorphic vegetable pots runs as an undercurrent through her work.

Kate's down-to-earth approach to ceramics reflects both her character and her background. She grew up in a home where traditional Staffordshire jugs and vases were brought out on special occasions and, without realising it at the time, she developed an instinctive liking for their broad, generous shapes. During her degree course at Bristol, the students were taken on two study trips to the industrial ceramic heartlands in Stoke-on-Trent. 'I wasn't consciously influenced by the pots I saw in museums,' she recalls, 'but somehow traditional English shapes suffused my concept of form. I love their stable, strong, forceful characteristics, especially their big, solid handles and proud spouts – perhaps because I recognise these features in myself. I think my work is very English in spirit in its profiles and curves.'

However, although her appreciation of Britain's industrial legacy is evident in the slip-cast jug shapes she designed for Stoke-based Moorland Pottery in 1987 (see page 39), as a practising potter Kate remains strongly attracted to the plasticity and physicality of clay itself. The low-cost Carnival Ware range (see pages 40-41) that she developed in her own studio, in which thrown vessels were manipulated and impressed while the clay was still soft, satisfied both her desire to create an affordable production range and her compulsion to 'play' with clay. 'I'm addicted to the

Andrew Logan as Host for The
Alternative Miss World, Earth, 1986

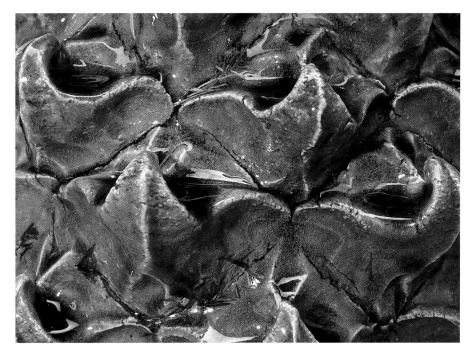

Detail of Choir Girl Pineapple, 1993.
The fired ceramic shows evidence that the clay was once soft, manipulated by the hand.

Pineapple teapot, Staffordshire (possibly Wedgwood), c.1765. h.14.6cm.

Schneeballen vase and cover, Meissen, late 19th century. h.56cm.

malleability of clay. I always respond to pots that show evidence of the human hand. It goes back to childhood memories of pressing soft pastry between finger and thumb to make the fluted rims on apple pies. I love traditional Brampton casseroles and mugs, because you can see and feel the indentation of the potter's thumb in the clay where a handle has been pressed into position. When I am using my fingers to model the flesh on my pineapple pots, it is this evidence of the human hand and the softness of clay that I am thinking about.'

Contrary to expectation, however, the choice of fruit and vegetables as her subject matter did not arise out of seeing 18th century Wedgwood pineapple wares – in the same way that her introduction to the work of Bernard Palissy post-dated her early work. 'My pineapple pots were inspired by the fruit itself, not by other pineapple pots. I don't think the craftsmen who modelled those early pineapple teapots were trying to create something new or opulent, they were simply responding to the exotic beauty of the pineapple itself, as I have.'

The one occasion on which Kate has been directly inspired by another ceramic genre is when she encountered the so-called Schneeballen vases made by the German porcelain factory Meissen. Schneeballen vases are conventional vessels transformed into something extraordinary by wild, rococo über-decoration. The 'snowballs' of the title are the giant baubles welded to their sides. In addition, scattered all over are thousands of tiny flower heads, laced with twining stems and dotted with birds. 'I love the complete absurdity of them. What appeals to me is the way this crazy sense of humour is expressed in such a seriously technical way.' Kate responded imaginatively to these bizarre vessels, which amongst other things acted as a catalyst in two separate ways. Firstly, and most obviously, they were responsible for the applied 'snowballs' that adorn her Mad Meissen Brussels Sprouts pots (see pages 131-9). As a secondary offshoot they prompted the massed sprigged daisies on her Millennium Jugs (see pages 69-71).

Being something of a maverick herself, Kate is naturally attracted to other artists and makers of a similar persuasion. Hence her reverence for the work of sculptor-jeweller Andrew Logan, who uses fragments of coloured mirrored glass to decorate

Shelf above Kate's workbench at Balls Pond Studio. A small pot by Axel Salto, dating from 1937, can be seen fourth from left.

Monica Young with her large coil-built stoneware vessels.

the surfaces of weird and wonderful creations large and small, ranging from the personal to the monumental. Logan is also the organiser of the legendary Alternative Miss World extravaganzas – a great excuse for dressing up on a grand scale (Kate herself has taken part on two occasions) – and the concept of transformation through fancy dress is fundamental to his work. Similarly, dressing up is perhaps the most illuminating analogy for Kate's treatment of the vessel form. She takes a naked coil-built or press-moulded vessel and dresses it up in a decorative sculptural coat, with layers of make-up added in the form of glazes.

A maverick sensibility, combined with a penchant for dressing up, also underlies the appeal of Kate's latest discovery, Axel Salto, a leading artist-potter active in Denmark during the mid 20th century. Salto created an astonishing series of knobbly stoneware pots in his studio at the Royal Copenhagen Porcelain Factory from the 1930s to the 1950s. His strongly organic pots, with their armour-like coats of irregular spiky protuberances and their milky-treacly glazes, have obvious parallels with Kate's work, particularly the way the decoration is scaled up or down to complement the form of the vessel. Although she only became aware of Salto's work fairly recently, his sculptural approach to the vessel clearly struck a chord, not to mention the sheer waywardness of his imagination. There are distinct differences, however, as Kate herself observes: 'Salto illustrates the "life force" in a male way; my aims, although similar, are decidedly female. It's a bit like the difference between Mother Nature and the Green Man.'

Kate is not one to be easily pigeon-holed, however, and she is perfectly capable of appreciating quiet, serene pots, such as those of Lucie Rie. Amongst her contemporaries she particularly admires Mo Jupp and Takeshi Yasuda, in both cases for their honest use of clay, and the way they exploit the unique sensibility and plasticity of the material to the full. She also has great respect for Janice Tchalenko, not only for her freedom in using glazes, but for her pioneering experimental attitude towards ceramics in general. Another heroine is Monica Young, who makes enormous, unglazed, coil-built vessels of great sculptural sophistication and grace. 'Very few potters are brave enough to work on this scale,' notes Kate. 'Monica Young is a great inspiration. Her pots highlight the importance of refining the form to its basic essence. By paring down the form she exaggerates it, in an Alice-in-Wonderland sort of way.' Parallels with fashion crop up in discussing Young's vessels, which are like statuesque female bodies swathed in a thick drape or robe. Although the bodies that Kate dresses are more Rubens-like than Modigliani-esque, the idea that the contours of the underlying form must be absolutely perfect before the body can be clothed is equally crucial to her work.

Kate clearly revels in the theatrical and couture aspects of dressing up her pots in different outfits, and the analogies with costume are more than just metaphorical. Living in London has given her a heightened awareness of the fashion industry, and brought her into close contact with several leading designers. The late Jean Muir

Dress designed by Zandra Rhodes.

14

Dried natural objects collected by Kate, used as source material.

Below centre:
Baby Bud Pumpkin Boxes,
1994 onwards.

Dried pumpkin stalks.

bought several pieces of her work, and Kate, conversely, is a devotee of Muir's loose-fitting jersey garments. Another fashion guru, Zandra Rhodes – 'my heroine in many respects,' says Kate – has collected her work for over fifteen years. Now close friends, the two have a mutual appreciation regarding the crossovers between fashion and ceramics. 'The relationship of fabric to the human body is similar to the relationship of applied decoration to a pot, so it seems logical to draw comparisons. My pots are naked bodies, which I dress up in various ways – sometimes with fake fur coats, sometimes with puffer jackets.' The aspect of Rhodes' work that Kate particularly admires is the union of form and surface in her custom-designed printed dress fabrics. 'Zandra has an amazing awareness of the way a garment hangs and moves, and how the contours of the body affect flat pattern, and vice versa. What I am trying to do with my pots is similar, to alter the scale of the pattern so that it relates to the contours of the vessel. You can also see this in all manner of natural phenomena – in flowers, for example, and in pine cones, the way they expand at the centre and are compressed at the top.'

Honing in on similarities between disparate aspects of material culture and the natural world is typical of Kate's openness to external stimuli. The urban and the rural appeal to her equally, an ambiguity reflected in the choice of the title The Allotment for her touring show. However, although Kate is responsive to an unusually wide range of things, the wonder of nature has clearly been her pre-eminent source of inspiration over the years. Wherever she travels she collects husks, cones and seedpods, which serve as inspiration for the bodies, coats and handles of her pots. Especially prized is her collection of pumpkin stalks. Her intimate knowledge of these specimens informs the diversity and delicacy of her pumpkin pot handles, particularly the suggestion of movement in the modelling of the stems.

Many of the ideas gleaned from her assorted collection of specimens are expressed in a generalised way, through subtle nuances of contour and texture. Sometimes though, a specific fruit, vegetable or nut prompts the creation a particular piece, as with her recent Sri Lankan Long Seed Pod. (See page 130.) Occasionally, chance 'finds' take on a landmark significance, prompting the exploration of major new creative themes. The discovery of a half baby coconut in its husk washed up on a beach in Venezuela was crucial to the development of her Sliced Fruits series, for example. (See pages 50-51 and page 85.) Durian fruit, pineapples, pine cones, blackberries and artichokes also link directly with the making of specific pieces.

Kate has travelled extensively since leaving college, devoting around two months each winter to visiting far-flung places with her partner Graham Inglefield, latterly accompanied by their daughter Scarlet. 'Going away gives me a perspective on what I am doing at home, and helps me to steer my direction with more clarity,' she explains. 'It's partly a respite from living in London – a way of keeping sane; but essentially a way of learning and broadening my horizons. India is a favourite, although it is very complex. The more I go, the less I seem to understand it. It is different to any other place on earth.' Over the years they have visited over thirty countries, including Sri Lanka, Thailand, Vietnam, Malaysia, Indonesia, Australia, New Zealand, Bahamas, Mexico, Peru, Venezuela, Ecuador, Cuba and the USA. Most of her trips are recorded in her travel diaries, lively annotated watercolour sketchbooks. (See pages 192-202) 'We have some great adventures. The travel diaries conjure up special moments so vividly. When I look at them, I can picture the whole scene. Travelling from town to town, visiting markets, temples and museums, studying the varied cultures, can be a sheer joy. I love the contrast between the ancient and the everyday.'

The buildings, sculptures and pots she encounters on these global trips have provided a regular stimulus for her own ceramics, although assimilation takes place mainly at a subliminal level, and there is not necessarily an obvious or immediate discernible result. 'It is more a process of accumulation, building up a subconscious library of creative visions and ideas.' Often it can be a tiny detail within a much larger work that triggers the most deep-rooted response. For example, in India she was fascinated by the ciment fondu spheres on the roofs of the derelict Mogul Palaces at Gujarat. These balls recall the appendages on her Mad Meissen Brussels Sprouts pots, while the temples roofs correspond with the lids on her pumpkin boxes.

'A lot of Indian sculpture and architecture conjures up ceramic associations for me, especially the stone columns carved out of solid rock in the caves at Ajanta, which look just like stacks of pots.' Buddhist icons have made a lasting impact over the years, and Kate is particularly interested in the carved stone sculptures of the Jain sect, whose proportions link mathematically to the human body. Her preoccupation with the inner life of the vessel can be traced back in part to the impact of a carved stone guardian creature at the entrance to a temple in Thailand. 'The figure holds a ball in its mouth, larger than the gap between its teeth, so it must have been carved from the stone inside the mouth itself,' she explains. 'I am fascinated by the idea of things inside things, a world within a world. Sometimes balls of clay are sealed inside my double-skinned pots to make them rattle, like seeds inside a dried fruit.'

Wherever she travels Kate tries to establish contact with local potters, sometimes discovering unexpected similarities with her own work. For example, the wavy frills on the large shallow jardinière bases seen at a production pottery outside Chaing Mai in northern Thailand recall the undulating shapes of her Carnival Wares and the rims of many of her larger pots. Kate's work reflects multiple associations, however, and there is rarely one simple, direct source for her ideas. A good example of how this indirect, subconscious stimulus occurs is provided by the monumental star-shaped carved stone bowls that she saw in Peru several years ago. Although by the time of her visit Kate had already produced the first of her Sliced Fruit of Your Dreams (see pages 50-51), seeing these sculptures at this stage appears to have reinforced her conviction about this form and triggered off further developments.

Kate is no purist in her response to the material world. Man-made objects – synthetic and natural – are just as likely to capture her imagination as a luscious

Stone carved creature guarding the steps at the entrance to a Buddhist temple, Thailand. The stone ball inside the mouth of the beast can be moved from side to side.

Derelict buildings, Gujarat, India.

Production pottery, Chaing Mai, North Thailand, showing wavy-rimmed pots relating to Kate's Carnival Ware.

N. 51 Museo Arqueológico incaico, Cuzco, Perú

Postcard from Museo Arqueologico, Cuzco, Peru, showing carved stone vessels that influenced Kate's Sliced Fruits.

Plastic rattles and other toys, Indian toys sold on the street; money box, and salt and pepper shakers.

Pink plastic hedgehog pet's toy. (below and centre left) The scale of the spikes in comparison to the body was crucial to the evolution of Kate's Tutti Frutti Bumper Car Jug.

Pumpkin-shaped wooden spice box carved from one piece of wood. Bought in Cochin, South India.

pineapple. Particularly valued amongst her global booty is a group collection of Indian street children's rattles, made of plastic and filled with rice, moulded in the form of fruit or leaves. Unlikely as it might sound, it was a pet's toy – a pink plastic hedgehog – that led to the evolution of her Tutti Frutti Bumper Car Jugs. It was not the object itself that inspired her; it was the relationship of surface decoration to the form. Having had an idea in the back of her mind for several years, she finally found the solution she was looking for in the proportions and arrangement of the spikes on this plastic pet's toy.

Kate's most prized possession is an antique pumpkin-shaped spice box carved from a single piece of wood, which Graham bought for her in Cochin in southern India. Her response to this object reveals a lot about her wider attitudes. 'I love the purity of the carving, the relationship of the stalk to the lid, and the way the lid fits. Although it is small, this pumpkin radiates a presence; it fills a much bigger space than it actually is.' This is what Kate aspires to in her work, and in fact it was this box that inspired her first crystalline-glazed pumpkin – Queen Pumpkin Box (see page 47 and front cover) – also diminutive in size, but large in spirit. People often mistakenly assume that, because her work is richly decorated and saturated with colour, it is somehow loud. In fact, the opposite is true; her pots are the embodiment of expressive understatement. 'Contained ebullience' is how Kate herself describes what she is aiming for, 'something inside the pot expanding, a life force bursting out.'

Until recently when Kate and Graham sold their house and decamped into a flat above Balls Pond Studio, many of the weird and wonderful objects collected on their global travels were housed in a specially constructed 'world cupboard' in their kitchen. (See page 18.) Built by Graham (a master craftsman who renovated the entire four-storey house, as well as constructing Balls Pond Studio itself), the internally illuminated, glass-fronted cupboard was inspired by his grandmother's china cabinet. Instead of housing porcelain tableware and seaside ornaments, however, it was crammed with a mélange of objects amassed on their annual rovings. 'When we are travelling I collect things automatically and instinctively, often only realising their full significance and associations later on. Then, when I am back at home working, I would

look in the world cupboard and get flashes of inspiration.' Although some items are valuable, the cheap and ephemeral are equally prized. While some objects are overtly beautiful, others fly in the face of accepted good taste. 'The juxtaposition between good taste and bad taste was exciting in itself. There was a carnival atmosphere in the world cupboard – it was a riot of colour – although each object was carefully placed.'

Sometimes it is everyday things closer to home that end up triggering a brainwave, as when Kate realised that the pointed oval light bulb used to illuminate the world cupboard itself was the perfect shape for the spikes on her Tutti Frutti Bumper Car Jug. (See page 17.) This was the first in a series of moulds created from different light bulbs, still a key feature in many of her recent appendage-laden pots. (See pages 122-39.) A light bulb superstore called Just Bulbs in New York provided rich pickings for her growing collection, along with an electrical shop in Hackney, where the bulb-enthusiast owner presented her with an array of vintage bulbs. In her on-going search for the perfect bauble, Kate has raided the bulbs on her own car: Volvo breaklights were used to create the moulds for the tiny berries on her Blackberry pots.

As a long-time observer of Kate's career (I first met her in 1987 in her start-up studio under the railway arches on the South Bank), it has been fascinating to watch her evolution. Although there are elements of continuity from one pot to the next, the rate of her development over the last fifteen years has been impressive by any standards. Most potters fall into more of a groove, and changes occur quite gradually. Kate's progress, by contrast, has been like a series of stepping stones, although hopefully she will never actually reach the other side. Every time I see a new batch of work, I think this must be as good as it gets. But then a few months later, she is on to the next thing, introducing a new element, cross-breeding a new hybrid or genetically engineering a different strain. However much water she draws from the well, it keeps

Shelf from the World Cupboard, formerly installed in the kitchen of Kate's house in Hackney, containing objects collected on her global travels.

on filling up again. It is not that Kate is restless, she just seems to find it so much fun.

As I write, Kate has just embarked on a new adventure. Over the last couple of years the potters who previously shared the facilities at Balls Pond Studio have gradually moved out, and the building has been converted into a live-work space. Having sold their house and moved into a flat above the London studio, she and Graham have now bought a property at Cotignac in Provence in the south of France, where they plan to spend half of their time. This change will inevitably influence the direction of Kate's future work, probably in dramatic ways. Exposure to new people, new landscapes and new vegetation – not to mention fresh produce in local markets – could have all kinds of repercussions. Malone-watchers such as myself can only wait with bated breath.

Whirlpool Alive Vase, 1986-7
h.60cm, w.42cm
Earthenware. Press-moulded
body, coil-built roll top neck,
applied press-moulded
sprigs. Coloured glazes,
glaze-fired six times.

The shoal of fish on the
surface of this pot spiral up
the body, swim under and
over the roll top, and down
into the interior of the
vessel. The wide cresting
rim – a recurrent form in
Kate's work at this date –
is intended to resemble a
breaking-wave. As a child
in the 1960s Kate was
often taken snorkelling in
Majorca, something she
adored. Drawing on these
memories, here she has
attempted to capture the
way shoals of fish move
with the flow of the water.

Previous page, *Fruits of the
Sea* 1986-7. Photograph by
Brian Nash for *The Observer*
Weekend Supplement 1987.

Starfish Flower Jar, 1987-8
h.54cm, w.42cm
Earthenware. Press-moulded
body, coil-built roll top neck,
applied press-moulded sprigs.
Coloured glazes, glaze-fired
four times.

Different coloured
earthenware glazes were
added to the main body in
each of the four glaze firings,
but the same blue glaze was
repeatedly applied to the roll
top rim. As a result the rim
takes on an astonishing depth
of colour, resembling the
appearance of deep blue glass.

Roll Top Shell Studded Vase,
1986-7
h.60cm, w.42cm
Earthenware. Press-
moulded body, coil-built roll
top neck, applied press-
moulded sprigs. Coloured
glazes, multiple glaze-fired.

As with many of Kate's
pieces, the base was made
by press-moulding, then the
top was hand-built with
coils. The same base mould
was used in the Whirlpool
Alive Vase and Starfish
Flower
Jar. 'The sprigged shells get
larger as the pot gets wider,
making the surface relate to
the form.'

On leaving the RCA, Kate
moved into the South Bank
Craft Centre, a communal
studio in the railway arches
under Hungerford Bridge
next to the Royal Festival
Hall, London. It was here
that her early Fruits of the
Sea pieces were made. The
centre provided rent-free
space and communal kiln
facilities to college leavers
for a maximum of one and a
half years, a stepping stone
to setting up a studio.
Although there was
unlimited free electricity, the
studios were very basic, with
none of the high-tech
facilities she had enjoyed at
college. It was here, largely
prompted by lack of
equipment, that Kate refined
her hand-building skills,
and developed the technique
of applying multiple layers
of glaze using a brush.
'Because we didn't have to
pay for electricity, it meant
that, if a pot didn't work, I'd
simply apply more glaze and
re-fire it until it improved.
Some pieces were fired up to
fifteen times. My style
evolved out of adversity.'

Aquarium Ginger Jar, 1987
h.52cm, w.42cm
Earthenware. Coil-built,
applied press-moulded sprigs
on body and lid, hand-built
handle and rims. Coloured
glazes, multiple glaze-fired.

'This piece illustrates fish in
an aquarium magnified as
they swim towards the glass.
The knob on the top is
deliberately askew because
the lid reminded me of a
bobble hat I wore as a child.'
The pot is decorated with
identical sprigged fishes of
six different sizes that relate
to the vessel's form. These
were made using a
traditional Stoke-on-Trent
technique called 'a shrink': a
hand-modelled clay fish was
used to create the original
plaster mould; a pressing
from this mould was fired,
shrinking in the process; the
smaller fish was then used to
make the next mould, and so
on, through six generations.

Caribbean Whirlpool Jug,
1989-90
h.38cm, w.35cm
Earthenware. Coil-built
body, hand-modelled relief
decoration. Coloured glazes,
multiple glaze-fired.

Produced for an exhibition at
Lyford Quay in the Bahamas,
this jug was made after
visiting the Van Gogh
Museum in Amsterdam.
Van Gogh's vibrant paint-
laden canvases clearly
influenced the brightly
coloured and clay – smeared
surface with its deliberately
overloaded glazes. In this
ceramic tour de force, not
only is the decoration
married to the form, but the
glaze is perfectly integrated
with the surface. 'Every time
a pot is re-fired, it causes the
glazes to slip down over the
form. This piece has a "lucky
drip" under the spout.'

Detail of raw clay on
Caribbean Whirlpool Jug,
1989-90
The gaping fish and paddling
squid on this vessel were
modelled by hand, without
the aid of tools or press-
moulds. The raw clay detail
shows how the creatures
were literally 'whipped up'
out of the soft clay.

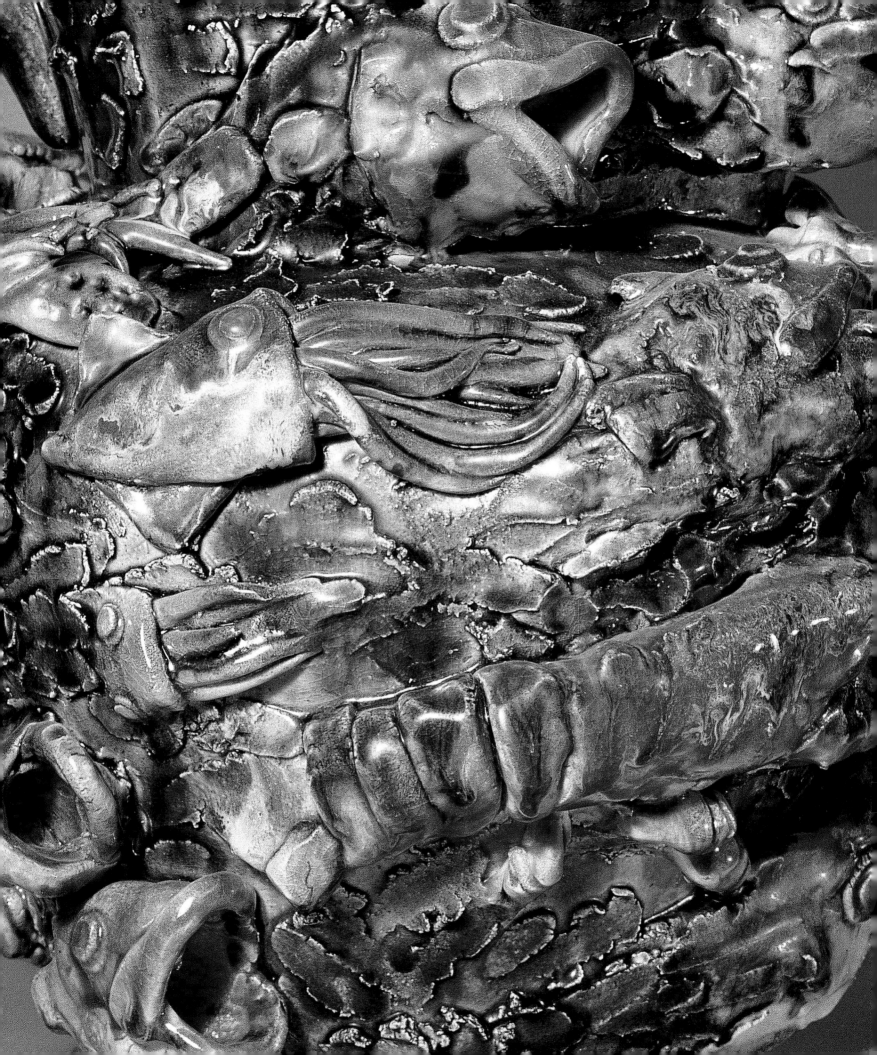

Sea Bed Alive Fruit Dish,
1990
h.32cm, w.48cm
Earthenware. Hand-built
and hand-modelled.
Coloured glazes, multiple
glaze-fired.

Although it ended as a dish,
there is no core vessel to this
aquatic piece, which was
conjured up from a myriad
of soft sculpted elements.
Kate makes the comparison
to coral or tree trunks,
which grow spontaneously,
suggesting their own form.
This piece, although
composed of a fish and a
lobster, has an abstract
quality. 'It was extremely
exciting to "discover" this
new process. It was only
later I became aware of the
parallels between my work
and that of Bernard Palissy.'

These remarkable hand-built
pieces, which defy the laws
of gravity, were constructed
little-by-little, day-by-day,
using temporary stilts to
support the overhanging
sections until the clay
stiffened enough to remove
them. 'The sea creatures on
the trunk weren't planned
in advance; they "grew"
spontaneously out of the
clay. The fluidity of the
modelling was a reaction
against the formal
characteristics of
coil-building. Camouflage is
the prevailing theme. When
you're underwater, you don't
immediately see things; it's
only when you stop and look
more carefully that the
mysteries are revealed.'

Detail of modelling and
glazes on *Sea Bed Alive Fruit*
Dish, 1990
Whether her subjects are
animal or vegetable, Kate has
the ability to bring her
creations to life by releasing
the dynamic potential of clay.

Deep Sea Candelabrum and
Fruit Dish, 1990
h.22cm, w.32cm
Earthenware. Hand-built and
hand-modelled. Coloured
glazes, multiple glaze-fired.

*Underwater Corals of Your
Dreams, 1990*
Various sizes: 8cm-30cm
Stoneware and stained parian
porcelain. Press-moulded and
hand-built. Various coloured
slips, high temperature glazes.

These fish tank accessories were
created as part of a large commission for the Otaru Maritimo
Hotel Restaurant in Japan
designed by Nigel Coates.

Kate also made an array of
serving dishes, display
platters, tiled trolleys and
water jugs for this project.
Because the fish tank
accessories were to be used
underwater, they could not
be made in earthenware, as
in warm salt water the low-
fired earthenware glazes
might have poisoned the
fish. As a result Kate was
forced to research higher

temperature bodies and
glazes. On consulting
Emmanuel Cooper's glaze
manual, one of the recipes
she came across was for a
crystalline glaze, which she
used on some of these pieces.
This initial experiment
triggered Kate's infatuation
with crystalline glazes, which
have subsequently become a
key feature of her work.

*Starfish Pie Dish, 1993-4
h.26cm, w.48cm*
Earthenware. Coil-built body,
hand-built handle and
spikes. Coloured glazes and
pebble glazes on exterior,
pebble glaze over a dry slip
on interior.
*Collection of The British
Council*

The eclecticism of Kate's
sources is apparent in this
piece: the shape was inspired
by Desperate Dan's Cow Pie
with its protruding horns,
and by Fenella Fielding's
remarkable waist and
hips in the film *Carry on
Screaming*. Like the Starfish
Jar, it alludes to the dangers
of the sea, hence the spiky
'underskirt' on the base,
each individual spike being
hand-made.

Starfish Jar, c.1992 h.34cm
Earthenware. Coil-built and
hand-built. Coloured and
pebble glazes.

'I made this piece after scuba
diving in the Bahamas,
when I learnt that it was
really quite scary in the sea,
with poisonous fish,
jellyfish and sharks.' The
vessel evokes some of the
darker aspects of marine
life, and the decoration
grows from the form. A
Crown of Thorns starfish,
tenaciously gripping a rock,

grows from the neck of the
pot. The nodules on the side
of the jar suggest the
suckers on octopus legs. In
this piece Kate experimented
with mottled 'special effect'
pebble glazes, and an
unplanned curtain of the
orange glaze dripped down
onto the blue body from the
starfish's legs. 'The vessel
has a rocking bottom, a
device seen on Indian and
Mexican domestic cooking
pots. This lifts the pot off
the ground, making it
appear to hover.'

*Mr and Mrs Deep Sea Meteor,
1987* h.30cm
Earthenware. Coil-built and
hand-built. Coloured glazes,
'Snowfall' glaze and transfer
prints.
Collection of Zandra Rhodes

'These pieces look like
meteors that have fallen
into the sea from space,
and become encrusted with
limpets and coral growth.
The male / female relationship
is important, especially the
contrast between the female
holes and male spikes.'

Mrs Deep Sea Meteor (right)
has a double skin, pierced
on the outside with 'port-
holes', revealing a shiny
pink secondary pot inside,
decorated with transfer
prints of Kate's drawings of
sea creatures. She is coated
with blistered, pigmented
'Snowfall' glaze, which puffs
up in the kiln. The name
'Snowfall' derives from the
fact that this glaze is used
in the ceramic industry in
Stoke-on-Trent to produce
the snow effects on
Christmas trees.

Neptune's Pillow, 1987
18cm x 34cm
Earthenware. Press-moulded.
Coloured glazes, multiple
glaze-fired.
Collection of The Mint
Museum of Craft and Design,
Charlotte, NC, USA.

Designed as a shallow fruit
bowl, this hollow pillow was
made in a two-part press

mould, the plaster mould
having been cast from a
coil-built master. Of the
fifteen or so pieces produced
in the series, all were
decorated with mottled
glazes. The glazes on this
piece, which include rutile
oxide, are particularly
spectacular. The glazes melt
over the contours of the pot
at the highest temperature.

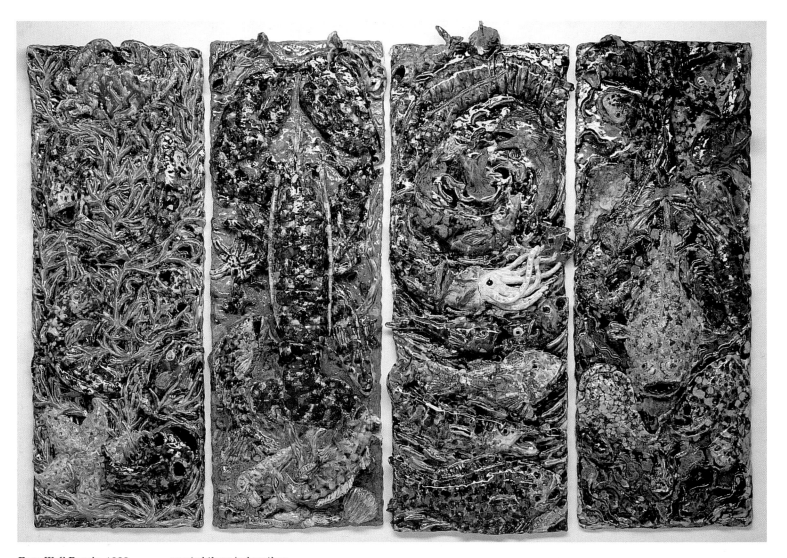

Four Wall Panels, 1988
Each panel: *120cm x 40cm*
Earthenware. Hand-built and
hand-modelled. Coloured
glazes and 'Snowfall' glazes,
multiple glaze-fired.

These panels were
commissioned by the
Marine Club for a
seafood restaurant, The
Quintessence Thameside
Restaurant in London.
Working to an extremely
tight deadline, Kate

created them in less than
seven weeks. She only had
access to the small kiln at
the South Bank studio, so
each panel had to be made
in four segments. The joints
were hidden beneath
overhanging sections of the
modelling, and the panels
were mounted on wooden
boards using flexible silicon.
Because the panels were
fired lying flat, the watery
glazes have pooled in the
recesses.

Opposite: Detail of *Larry the
Lobster and Whirlpool
Panels, 1988*
'Modelled from a lobster
I bought at Billingsgate
Market at dawn.'

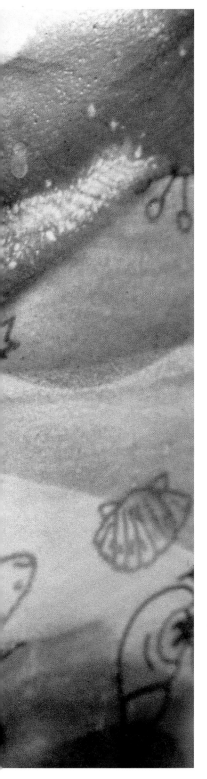

Undersea Jug, 1985 h.34cm
Earthenware. Press-moulded. Transfer prints and coloured glazes, multiple glaze-fired.

Produced at the Royal College of Art, this large jug was press-moulded using a plaster mould taken from a coil-built original. The hollow handle was press-moulded separately, then applied. The decoration was partly the result of a happy accident. Yellow glaze was applied first of all, followed by the transfer-printed fish. Disliking the result, Kate dabbed on further coloured glazes, thinking that the transfers would burn away during the next glaze firing. In fact the enamel transfers became trapped and distorted between the glazes, so she added more, resulting in unusual multi-layered effects.

Deep Sea Range, Moorland Pottery, 1987
Maximum. *h.20cm*
Earthenware. Slip-cast. Sponged (left and right), stamped (right) and painted (right) underglazes, clear glaze. Twice-fired coloured glazes (centre).

Kate designed both the shapes and the decoration for this range of production wares, which was manufactured until 1993. The wide neck and generous handle are typical of her approach to the jug form. Keen to translate her designs into affordable low-cost wares, she approached Moorland Pottery because they were one of the few remaining small Stoke-on-Trent firms who still used skilled hand decorators. The jug on the far right has the most complex decoration: hand-registered rubber stamps were applied over sponged colour, while the rim, foot and handle were brush banded by hand.

Detail of *Undersea Jug, 1985*

Carnival Ware Vase, 1999
h.18cm
Earthenware. Wheel-thrown,
manipulated and impressed.
Twice-fired coloured glazes.

Kate's Carnival Ware,
produced periodically up to
the present, marks her second
attempt to create a range of
modestly priced production
wares. This time, instead of
working with a factory, she
employed a thrower (mostly
Nick Membery) to throw
shapes to her designs. Kate
then pushes and pulls the soft
clay, using a variety of found
implements and homemade
plaster stamps to impress
simple patterns. Buttons,
beads, brooches, pen lids,
plastic toys and seeds have
all been deployed at various
times. Although the glazes
look as though they have been
applied at random, each colour
has, in fact, been carefully
positioned according to its
character- istics, to highlight
aspects of the form and to
complement the impressed
markings on the pot.

Carnival Ware, 1994 onwards
Various sizes: *10-20cm*
Earthenware. Wheel-thrown,
manipulated and impressed.
Twice-fired coloured glazes.

Detail of *Mother Pumpkin Bowl*,
c.1992-3
h.24cm, w.57cm
Stoneware. Coil-built.
Crystalline glazes.

Mother Pumpkin Bowl, a coil-built vessel with a double skin, was one of Kate's earliest large crystalline-glazed pots. Her expansion into this new area prompted her to carry out a whole series of glaze tests. This piece is decorated with a variety of experimental glaze tests, daubed on the biscuit-fired vessel using a big soft brush, then once glaze-fired. Crystalline glazes become much runnier in the kiln than earthenware glazes, more like the consistency of milk than syrup. Here the glaze has pooled in the well of the vessel, producing a turquoise lake.

Mother Pumpkin Jug,
1990-1
h.42cm, w.64cm
Earthenware. Coil-built body, hand-built handle. Coloured glazes, including tin glazes, multiple glaze-fired.
Collection of the Crafts Council

'Mother Pumpkin Jug – my first vegetable pot – was made following a trip to Mexico, where I saw beautiful pumpkins in the markets. I also fell in love with the lily paintings of Diego Rivera, and these influenced the lily-like quality of the neck. The inside of the jug is decorated with a vivid, luminous turquoise glaze, inspired by the *ahebas* (water wells) in southern Mexico.' Because this is such a large piece, the handle was cut in half, hollowed out and rejoined, to prevent it exploding in the kiln.

Mother Pumpkin Bowl, c.1992-3

*Choir Boy and Choir Girl
Pineapples, 1993
Right: h.18cm, w.20cm*
Stoneware. Press-moulded
body, coil-built neck, hand-
built handle and rims,
applied hand-modelled
surface decoration.
Crystalline glazes.

'These were some of the first
pieces where I "dressed" a
plain vessel in a decorative
"costume" or "coat". When

I look at them now, the
segments on the body
remind me of "Tudor"
breeches, where cloth
from an undergarment is
pulled through slits from
underneath. The Choir Boy
on the left has a traditional
ruff, just like the choir boys
on Christmas cards.'
    Although real pineapples
provided the inspiration for
the applied decoration on
these pots, the modelling

is intensely sculptural,
a direct response to the
malleability of soft clay.
Each segment is hand-built
using a standard formula
of movements. First a
pyramid of clay is joined
to the surface of the pot,
before being pushed,
squeezed and pinched into
shape. Pools of glaze, caught
in the cupped segments,
emphasise the detail of the
modelling. 'Initially I wasn't

aware of the symbolism
of the pineapple, although
I later learnt that it sym-
bolised hospitality and
prosperity. It was the sheer
beauty of the fruit that
inspired these pieces.'

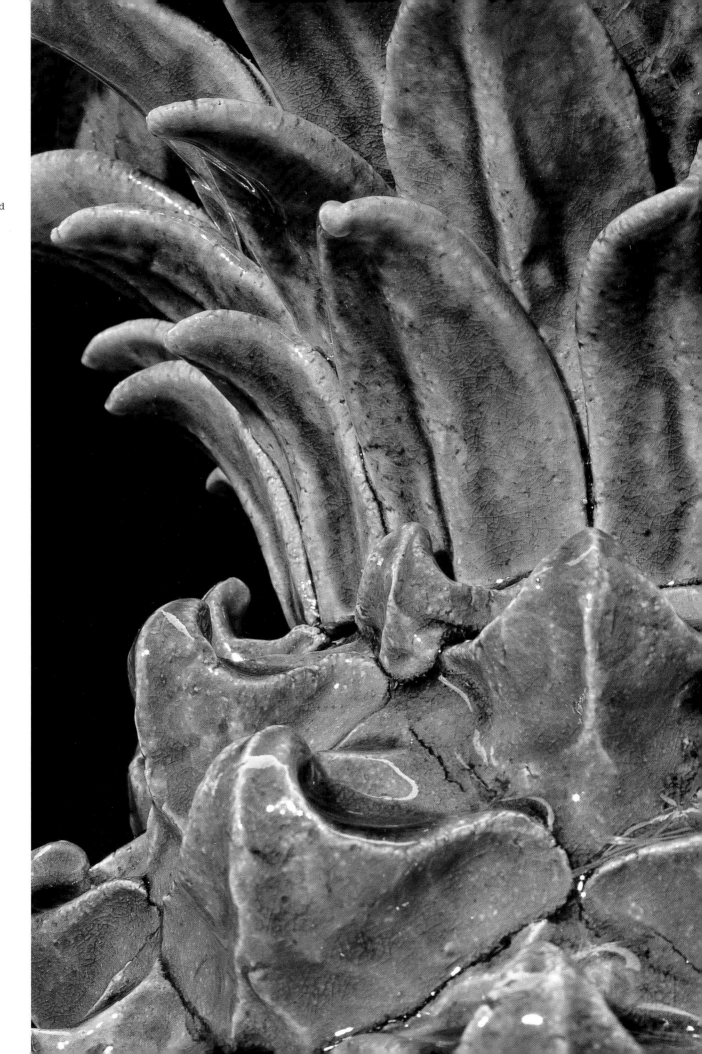

Detail of modelling and glazes on *Choir Girl Pineapple*, 1993

Cinderella's Carriage, 1996
h.28cm; w.44cm
Stoneware. Coil-built body
and lid, hand-built handles
and spout.
Crystalline glazes.
Collection of Brighton
Museum and Art Gallery

The crystal formations in
crystalline glazes vary
enormously in their size,
structure and disposition,
depending on the glaze
recipe, the firing cycle, and
the shape of the piece. On
this teapot a dense matrix of
fine crystals has grown on
the shoulder of the vessel.

*Queen Pumpkin Box, 1993
h.32cm, w.26cm*
Stoneware. Coil-built body
and lid, hand-built handle.
Crystalline glazes.

It's a great challenge to
make the lid of a clay box
fit properly, especially
when firing to stoneware
temperatures, where the
clay distorts and shrinks
more than at earthenware

temperatures. Kate's method
is to make the body, place
cling film across the opening
to keep the two pieces
separate, then coil-build
the lid on top. Once the lid
is firm enough, it is lifted
away, and a narrow coil of
soft clay is added to its rim.
The lid is then squeezed
back against the opening
of the body, with a cling
film divide. The added coil

strengthens the edge of
the lid, giving it a 'gallery
lip', whilst at the same
time ensuring that the lid
and body are intimately
registered. The stalk handle
is created by pinching,
squeezing, and gently easing
a twist into the soft clay.
'Working out the correct
proportion of the handle
to the pot is very difficult,
not least because the handle

shrinks less in volume than
the main body in the kiln.'
    Queen Pumpkin Box is
remarkable not only for the
delicacy of its shape, but for
the quality of its crystals,
which resemble tiny
pompoms. The electric blue
crystals contrast sharply
with the honey-coloured
base. Black nickel oxide
added to the glaze triggered
these striking effects.

Information about
crystalline glazes is provided
in the techniques section of
the book. In brief, crystals
are grown during the
controlled cooling cycle
of a glaze firing because
the glaze solution becomes
over-saturated. The closest
analogy is to cooking jam
or toffee, where sugar
crystals form if the molten
fluid is over-boiled.

*Prince Pineapple, c.1993
h.39cm*
Stoneware. Coil-built body,
hand-built handle and rim,
applied hand-modelled
surface decoration.
Crystalline glazes.

The applied decoration
exaggerates the shape of
the vessel, making it seem
more dynamic. The diamond-
shaped segments relate
closely to the form, swelling
in size towards the shoulder,
shrinking towards the foot.

Golden Lady Gourd, 1994
h.36cm
Stoneware. Press-moulded
body, hand-built neck.
Crystalline glazes.

Red iron oxide was added
to a Derek Clarkson base
glaze to create the blanket of
crystals on this pot. Note the
pinky colour on the shoulder
where the glaze is thinner.

Detail of glazes on neck of
Golden Lady Gourd, 1994

'I deliberately made the
narrow top flat rim of the
neck slightly concave so that
the glaze would pool. This
intensifies the colour and
draws attention to the star-
shaped rim. Small amounts
of green glaze have run
down the valleys below the
neck, emphasising the form.
I love the way this happens.
It's subtle details like this
that make a piece complete.'

*Sliced Sun Fruit of Your
Dreams, c.1990*

Detail of glaze on the rim of
*Sliced Sun Fruit of Your
Dreams, c.1990*
d.44cm
Earthenware. Press-
moulded, carved on the rim.
Coloured and pebble glazes.

'With this piece I was trying
to suggest the idea of a fruit
being sliced open to reveal
the sun shining inside.
The basic shape was press-

moulded in two parts, then
the outline of the sun was
carved back in low relief on
the top surface. This was an
early use of pebble glazes.
The sun was created by
using a rosso red glaze
under a yellow pebble glaze.
I enjoy the way these glazes
oozed over the rim and along
the details like slow-flowing
tongues of molten lava,
stopping at the perfect place.'

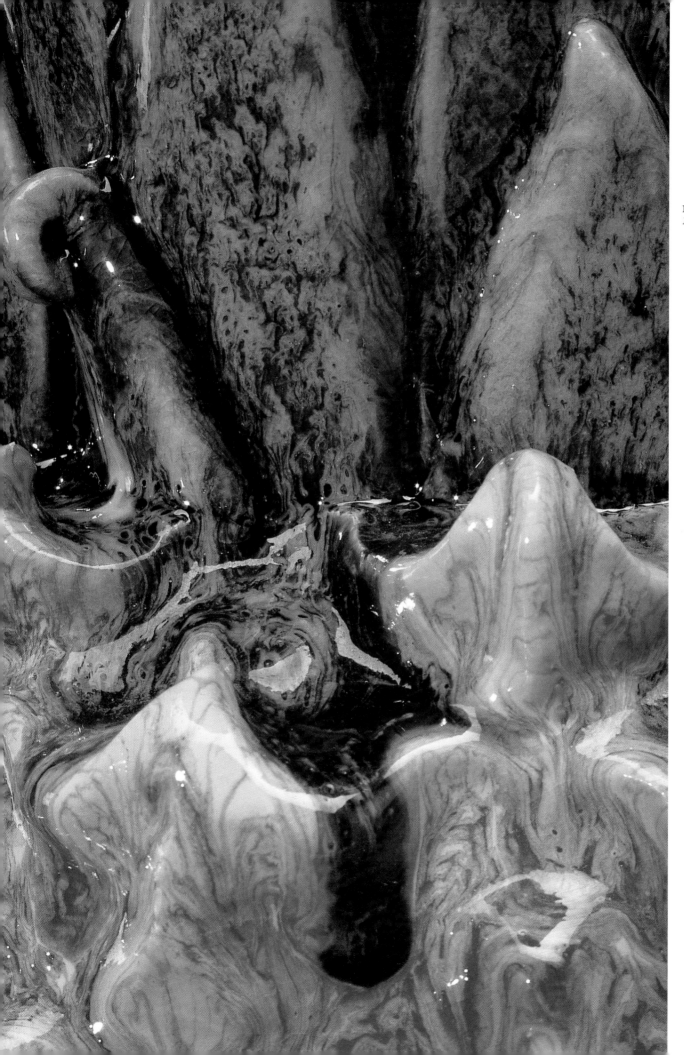

Detail of glazes on
Pineapple on Fire, 1993

Pineapple on Fire, 1993-4
h.48cm
Earthenware. Wheel-thrown body, coil-built neck, hand-built handle and rim, applied hand-modelled surface decoration. Coloured and pebble glazes, multiple glaze-fired.

'This pot was inadvertently over-fired during its third glaze firing, a happy accident which prompted me to push pebble glazes to the limit in terms of layering and firing. In the end I gave the piece five more glaze firings, and the last three were deliberately over-fired. The effects are extraordinary. The pebble glaze came alive and moved, resulting in a crazy type of marbling. This created a really strong relationship between glaze and surface. The leaves on the neck look as though light is shining on them where the green glaze has moved downwards, revealing the yellow and green mottled glaze tips beneath.'

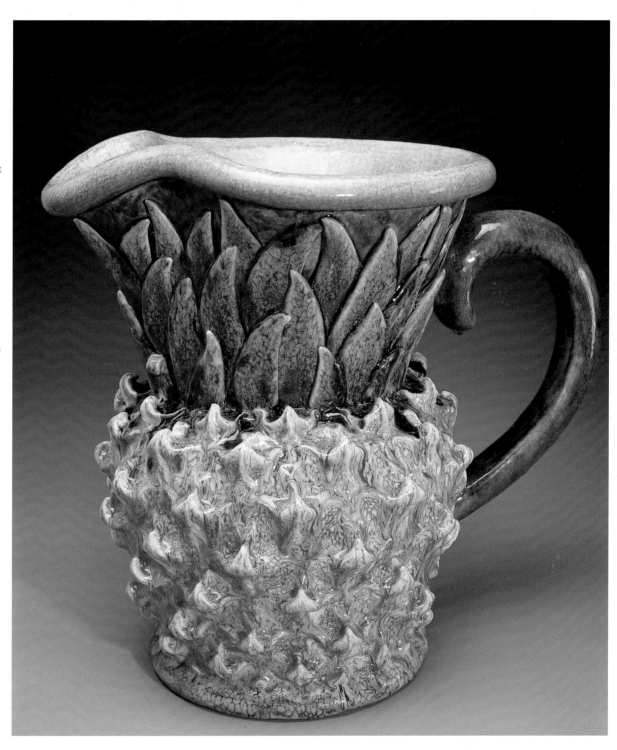

Mother Pineapple Epergne,
1996
h.34cm, w.74cm
Stoneware. Coil-built and
hand-built body, hand-
pinched and hand-built baby
pineapples, applied hand-
modelled surface decoration.
Crystalline glazes.
Collection of the British
Council

This epergne was
commissioned by the British
Council for a touring
exhibition called *Dish of*
the Day. It formed the
centrepiece of a giant table
setting, each component
made by a different British
potter. When Kate visited a
pineapple farm in Australia,
she noticed that during
harvesting lots of tiny
'satellite' pineapples were
pulled off from the foot of

the main fruit. Co-opting
this idea for her epergne,
she indulged in a bit of
artistic licence by attaching
the 'babies' to the hips. Kate
was pregnant with her
daughter Scarlet at the time
she made this vessel, so
motherhood was naturally
on her mind. This piece
consciously evokes the
broadness and weight of
a pregnant woman.

This image was used on the
poster *Dish of the Day*.

Father Pineapple Bowl, 1996
w.64cm
Stoneware. Coil-built and
hand-built body, applied
hand-modelled surface
decoration. Crystalline
glazes.

When Kate receives an
important commission, she
starts out by making two
pieces. Partly a safeguard
in case of accidents, this also
gives her the freedom to
choose which one to carry
through at a halfway stage.
This oval bowl is the spouse
to the Mother Pineapple
Epergne (see opposite).

Mae West Pumpkin, c.1992
w.44cm
Stoneware. Coil-built body,
hand-built handle.
Crystalline glazes.

'This pot – the most buxom
of pumpkins – is all bosoms,
cleavages and bottoms.
It has a belly button
underneath.' Rounded 'belly
button' bases are a common
feature of Kate's gourds and
pumpkins. They are created
by resting a slab of soft clay
on a sheet of cling film, then
placing this over a stilt in
the centre of a bowl mould,
so that it sags around the

stilt. Once the clay has
stiffened, the walls of the
vessel are coil-built upwards,
using a piece of soft foam as
a cushion on which rest the
pot while it is being made.
'When you open the box, the
inside of the reversed belly
button looks like a volcano,
with deep pools of crystals
that relate beautifully to
the form.'

Queen Pineapple, 1994-5
h.69cm
Stoneware. Wheel-thrown
body, coil-built neck, applied
hand-modelled surface
decoration. Crystalline glazes.

This pot demonstrates the
way Kate constantly varies
and develops her chosen
themes. No two pineapples
are the same. Although in
no way anthropomorphic,
her pots often assume
human characteristics.
Here, the maturity and
wisdom of age are suggested
by the amount of foliage on
the attenuated neck.

*Triumphant Pineapple, 1996
h.52cm*
Stoneware. Wheel-thrown
body, coil-built neck, hand-
built roll-top rim, applied
hand-modelled surface
decoration. Crystalline
glazes.

Kate constantly experiments
with scale, particularly the
relationship between the size
of the vessel and the scale of
the relief decoration on the
surface. The diamonds on this
pot are larger than usual, as
though a smaller, younger
pineapple has been enlarged.
The glazes demonstrate
Kate's increasing mastery
in applying and firing
crystalline glazes. Two glazes
of a similar honey tone
(mottled nickel oxide and
red iron oxide) are used on
the main body, interacting
with each other, enlivening
the surface and giving it
depth. The pale turquoise
glaze on the interior of the
neck was chosen to suggest
light radiating from within.
This glaze contains a small
amount of copper, as does
the green glaze on the leaves.
Iron oxide is the colouring
agent for the honey coloured
glaze running in streaks
down the neck. Turquoise
glaze has also run down in
stripes from the lip. 'I like
it when the kiln takes over.
Having the knowledge of how
glazes will move and run very
much dictates the forms and
surfaces I make and the way
I glaze them.'

*Prince Gourd Jug, c.1998
h.34cm*
Stoneware. Press-moulded
body, hand-built neck and
handle. Crystalline glazes.

Created from a mould taken
from a coil-built master, this
piece has a rounded 'belly
button' base. 'This is my
favourite gourd jug. I really
concentrated when making
the handle. I have observed
the way the stem of a horse
chestnut leaf swells slightly
where it joins the branch. I
tried to suggest this at the
base of the handle. The scroll
at the top was inspired by a
giant elaborate Baroque jug
in the entrance at the Musée
d'Orsay in Paris.'

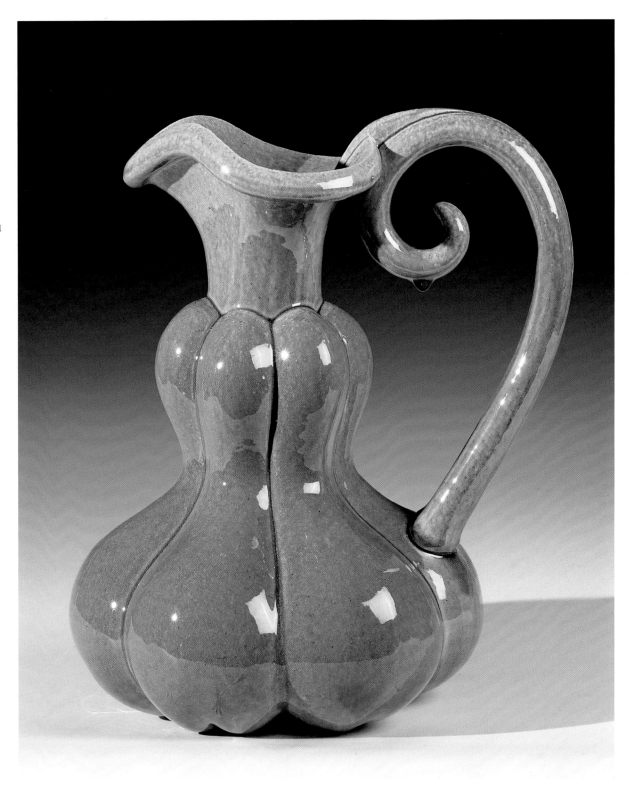

Mother Pumpkin, 1993
h.46cm, w.40.5cm
Stoneware. Press-moulded
body and lid, hand-built
handle. Crystalline glazes.

Prompted by the buxom coil-
built Mae West Pumpkin,
this ebullient press-moulded
pumpkin was serial-produced
in an edition of twenty,
with two artist's proofs, in
crystalline glazes. With its
full generous curves, precise
detailing, and ebullient
profile, it symbolises Mother
Nature, representing a ripe
fruit at its peak of perfection.
Each piece in the edition is
individualised by the modelling of the handle and the
choice of glazes. On the outside are just a few isolated
crystals, but the inside is
laden with a heavy matrix
of giant crystals, like a jewel
box lined with velvet. 'There
is a fine line between kitsch
glitziness and extreme
delicacy. I prefer to use fewer,
smaller crystals on the
exterior so that they don't
muddle the lines. My aim is
to create a harmony and
balance between form and
surface so that the crystals
don't overpower the form.'

Detail of handle, lid and glazes on *Mother Pumpkin*, artist's proof, 2001

The spiralling handle is like a wisp of thought emerging out of someone's head. Crucial to the success of the piece as a whole, the handle requires intense concentration to create. Every minute detail has to be exactly right – the width, the length, the taper, the coil, the flow. 'If the clay is too soft, it will droop; if it's too dry, it will crack and crumble, so choosing the correct consistency of clay is vital before making a start. Whereas other making techniques are slow, and mistakes can be corrected to a certain extent, the handle has to be hand-built in a single, uninterrupted stint. It requires a very intense, concentrated two hours for each one.'

Baby Bud Pumpkin Boxes,
1994 onwards
Even though they are
produced from the same
mould, the combination
and disposition of the

glazes individualises the
character of each pumpkin.
The 'pips' on the shoulder
and the lid indicate how the
two should be registered to
make the lid fit.

Baby Bud Pumpkin Box,
1994 onwards
h.24cm, w.24
Stoneware. Press-moulded
body and lid, hand-built
handle. Crystalline glazes.

This is a smaller version
of Mother Pumpkin, with a
rounded 'belly button' base.
'I love the bud-like quality of
these small pumpkins, like
the curves on babies' bodies.'

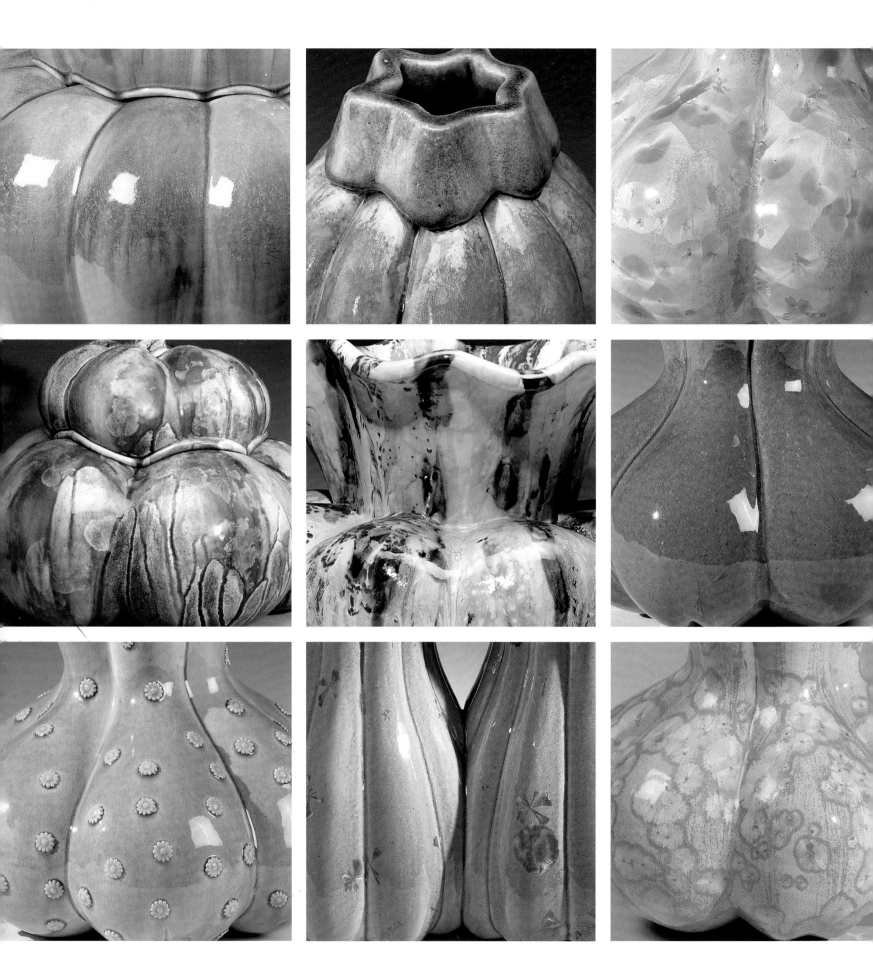

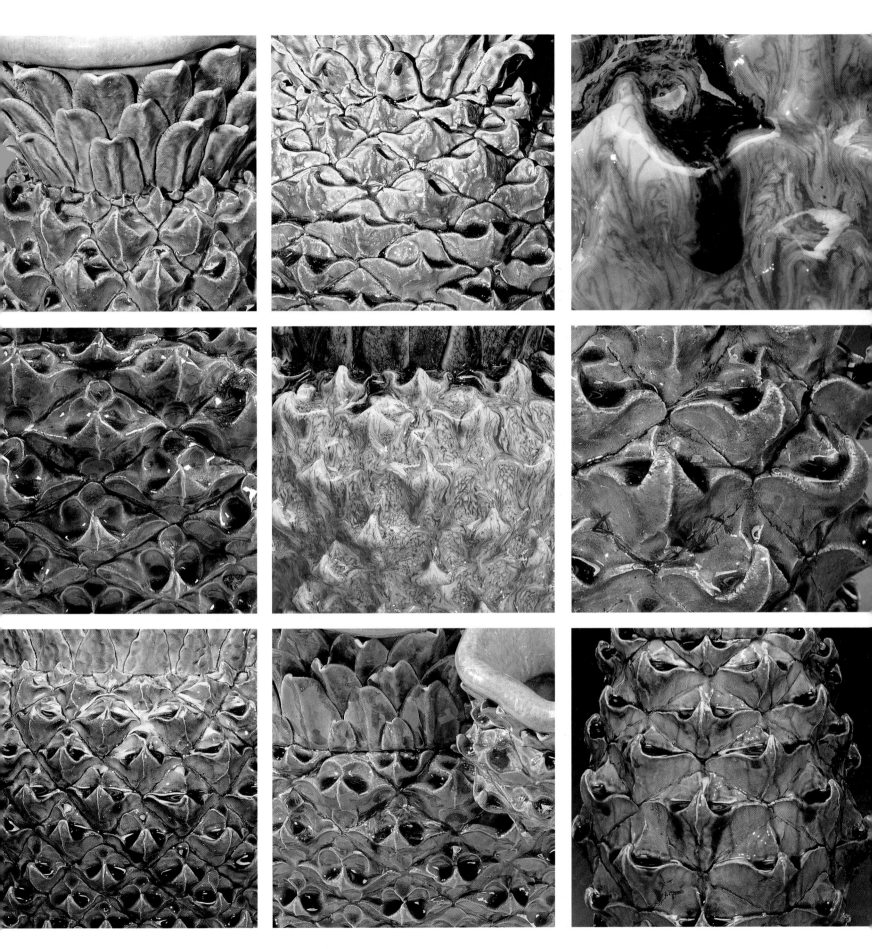

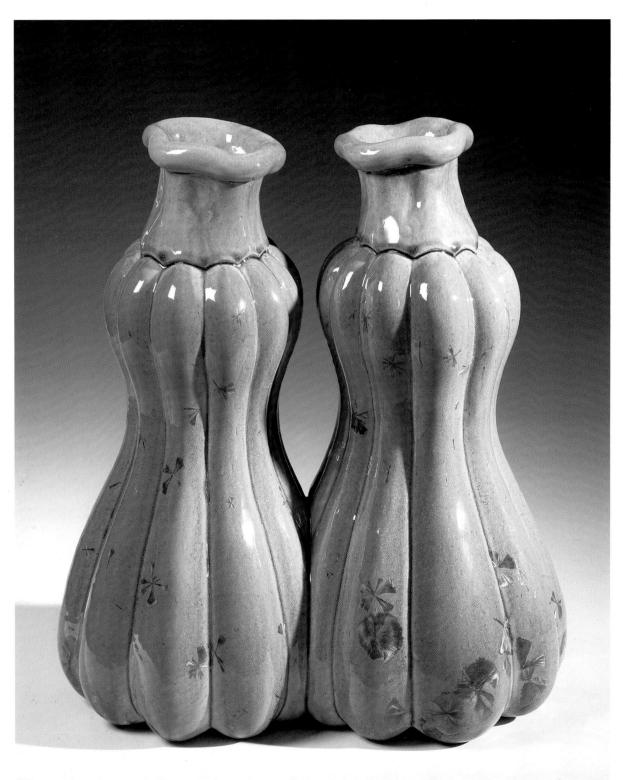

Siamese Twins, 1995
h.36cm
Stoneware. Press-moulded bodies, coil-built necks, joined at the base. Crystalline glazes.

Whereas Kissing Couple touch at two points, these gourds are only joined at the base. The relationship between the two vessels is crucial in both cases, not only where and how they merge, but the space in between them

Kissing Couple, 1998
h.32cm, w.42cm
Stoneware. Press-moulded
bodies, coil-built necks, cut
and joined at the lip and
body. Crystalline glazes

Visiting museums in Mexico
and Peru, Kate became
interested in Pre-Columbian
composite vessels in
which separate chambers
were welded together.
This, combined with her
enthusiasm for the weird
real-life double-vegetables,
fed directly into this piece.
'The unbroken curve on the
inside of the neck resembles
a human lip, hence the name
Kissing Couple.' The gourd
on the right has a 'lucky
drip' sticking up on its
shoulder where the dark
green glaze has dropped
down from the rim, but not
melted as usual; its partner
has a drip of unmelted glaze
hanging down under its lip.

Daisy Lady Gourd, 1999
h.36cm
Stoneware. Press-moulded body, coil-built and hand-built neck, applied press-moulded sprigs. Crystalline glazes.

Silver Lady Gourd and Beige Lady Gourd 1995 and 1996
h.36cm
Stoneware. Press-moulded body, coil-built and hand-built neck. Crystalline glazes.

Silver Lady Gourd, Big Crystal Lady Gourd and Daisy Lady Gourd were produced using the same basic mould, but with different glazes on each piece. In each case the honey-coloured glaze placed on the rim has dribbled down the neck, while the green glaze originally applied on the neck has completely slipped off, leaving only traces behind.

Garland Jug for the Millennium, 1999
h.34cm
Stoneware. Press-moulded body and handle, made separately. Applied press-moulded, impressed and hand-modelled, sprigged and carved straps. Crystalline glazes.

Late 18th century English transfer-printed creamware jugs provided the inspiration for the Millennium Jug series. 'I love the robust forms of those everyday commemorative pots, particularly the way emblems of work, such as farm implements, are used as decoration.' Although Kate's pieces are sprigged rather than printed, she has decorated them with her own personal emblems of productivity and creativity: pumpkins, pineapples, gourds and flowers. The jug itself – for Kate a symbol of friendship and the family – is also employed as a motif. The daisies are mounted on a raised 'platform' so that the heart appears to be bursting out.

Millennium Meadow
Sprigged Jug, 1999
h.34cm
Stoneware. Press-moulded
body and handle, made
separately then joined and
extensively hand-worked.
Applied press-moulded,
impressed and hand-
modelled sprigs.
Crystalline glaze.

In recent years Kate has
been amazed by Meissen
Schneeballen vases –
wild rococo porcelain
concoctions, ornamented
with thousands of tiny
flowers. The sprigged
daisies on her Millennium
Jugs were inspired by these
massed floral effects. The
mould for the daisy sprig
was made from a plastic
earring bought in Spain.

Detail of sprigging on
Millennium Meadow
Sprigged Jug, 1999

The level of detail on
this piece is remarkable.
'Applying the daisy sprigs
was incredibly labour
intensive and fiddly. I made
a small patch each day,
while the piece was kept
wrapped in cling film to
prevent it drying out. I
usually keep pots damp
with a fine water spray, but
with the daisies being so
fine, they would have lost
their definition. This made
the job very difficult.'

Three Millennium Mugs,
1999
h.12cm, w.22cm
Stoneware. Wheel-thrown
stoneware body, hand-built
or plaited handles. Applied
press-moulded, impressed
and hand-modelled sprigs,
stamped lettering.
Crystalline glazes.

Kate was one of several
leading potters invited by
Galerie Besson in London
to contribute to an exhibition
of Millennium Mugs. For
the lettering she used an
alphabetical typeface from
leather punches. The handle
on the mug in the centre was
made of soft coils of plaited
clay. The other two have
'worm' handles, created by
rolling a coil of clay under
a metal comb, bending it
into the correct shape, then
joining it to the mug.

Millennium Symbols Jug,
1999
h.28cm
Stoneware. Press-moulded
body. Applied press-moulded,
impressed and hand-modelled
sprigs, stamped lettering.
Crystalline glazes.

'Whereas the gourds I've
made have pronounced
hips and exaggeratedly
thin necks, suggesting the
female form, these jugs are
decidedly male in character,

with their broad shoulders
and thick, bullish necks.
Flimsy handles make me feel
nervous about picking up
a pot. Although primarily
decorative, I want my jugs
to look strong enough to use,
which is why I emphasise
their robust handles.' The
words 'Fertility, Hospitality,
Prosperity and Sharing' are
stamped around the foot –
a gesture of optimism for
the next thousand years.

Lady Daisy Jug, 1999
h.28cm
Stoneware. Press-moulded
body, applied press-moulded
sprigs. Crystalline glazes.

The crystals on the body
of this jug perfectly complement the sprigged
daisies. Crystals are like
seeds, in many ways, which
makes the use of crystalline
glaze particularly relevant
to the theme of nature
and growth.

Flying Pineapple Jug, 1998
h.28cm
Stoneware. Press-moulded
body, applied press-moulded
sprigs. Crystalline glazes.

The lop-sided flying
pineapples on this piece
are reminiscent of flying
ducks. The feathering of
the crystalline glazes on
the neck recalls the texture
of pineapple flesh.

Artichoke Jug, 1997-8
h.32cm
Stoneware. Press-moulded.
Crystalline glazes.

'I've been striving to capture
the essence of the artichoke
shape for years; so far it
has proved elusive. This
piece was completely press-
moulded, including the
leaves and the handle. The
mould is complicated and
extremely difficult to use,
but somehow this seems
rather appropriate as the
artichoke is a symbol of
tenacity.'

Stag Horn Coral Bumper Car Jug, 1989
h.25cm, w.36cm
Stoneware. Press-moulded body, press-moulded handle, applied hand-modelled surface decoration. Crystalline glazes.

Produced towards the end of Kate's Fruits of the Sea period when she was starting to experiment with crystalline glazes, this piece marked the advent of a new series of chunky oval jugs with thick rolled lips and feet, reminiscent of fairground bumper cars.

The foot roll gives a feeling of stability; the wide mouth suggests a gaping fish.
'Of all the jug shapes I have made, this is my favourite – it is generous and secure. I have used this base mould for over a decade. Each jug is dressed in its own customised coat.'

Durian Fruit and Buddhist Swirl Bumper Car Jugs, 1992
h.25cm, w.36cm
Stoneware. Press-moulded body, press-moulded handle, applied hand-modelled surface decoration. The prickly coat of the Durian Fruit Jug (left) was created by rolling and pinching variously sized balls of soft clay, with the base of each spike being scratched and wetted before being pushed onto the body. By alternating bands of large and small spikes, the surface appears to undulate, just like the durian fruit itself.

The wavy lines on the *Buddhist Swirl Jug* (right) were inspired by the carved drapery on Buddhist icons in Sri Lanka. This pattern also recalls the ripples left in the sand by the receding tide. Because the glaze has collected in the undulations, vertical stripes are produced where the melted glaze runs downwards.

Detail of spikes and handle
on *Durian Fruit Bumper
Car Jug*, 1992

Detail of *Buddhist Swirl
Bumper Car Jug*, 1992

Tutti Frutti Bumper Car Jug, 1997
h.27cm, w.40cm
Earthenware. Press-moulded body, press-moulded handle, press-moulded applied bulbs. Coloured and pebble glazes. *Collection of The J.B. Speed Art Museum, Louisville, Kentucky (Partial and promised gift, Adele and Leonard Leight Collection)*

'A small pink plastic hedgehog (see page 17) inspired the "coat" on this jug, and the mould for the spike was taken from a pointed light bulb. Each hollow press-moulded spike is individually squeezed to shape so that the spikes seem to be cuddling up to each other. The sense of squeezing together and at the same time bursting out, is what makes this my favourite piece. Tutti Frutti is about the essence of a seed and growth; it's also about fake fur coats, 1960s swimming caps and Cadbury's chocolate mini eggs!'

Detail of pebble glazes on *Tutti Frutti Bumper Car Jug, 1997*

*Family Group of Tutti
Fruttis, 2000
Maximum h.37cm*
Earthenware. Press-moulded
body, press-moulded handle,
press-moulded applied bulbs.
Coloured and pebble glazes.

Kate often creates comp-
lementary male and female
pots. Here, the tall wife and
bumper car jug husband
are accompanied by a child.
Each of the bulbs used to
decorate these pieces is

press-moulded individually.
To prevent them exploding
during firing, they are
either pierced with several
holes around the edge or
with one big breather hole
into the body.

Detail of *Family Group of Tutti Fruttis*, 2000

*Lilac Heart Sliced Fruit
of Your Dreams, 1998
h.20cm, d.38cm
Earthenware. Coil-built
with double skin. Coloured
and pebble glazes on interior,
pebble glazes over a dry
black slip on exterior.*

Giant Sliced Fruit of Your Dreams, 1994
h.34cm, d.52cm
Earthenware. Coil-built with double wall. Coloured and pebble glazes on interior, pebble glazes over a dry slip on exterior.

This double-walled vessel was coil-built in two stages. The lobed interior was made first, then the pot was inverted on a flat board and the rim added. At this stage it looks like a bowler hat. Next, the outer skin was coiled back up around the inner bowl and sealed over the top, leaving a hollow between the two layers. (See pages 184-5 for illustrations of a pea pod being made using this technique.)

The basic ready-made pebble glaze that Kate uses is white. She customises it by adding various colouring agents. The remarkable colour and texture effects she achieves are created by applying pebble glazes over layers of plain coloured glazes and slips – the result of her extensive programme of glaze testing. On this piece, for example, the interior is decorated with a yellow pebble glaze over a rosso red glaze. The rim has a green pebble glaze over a blue glaze, with a thin band of

lilac around the outer edge to suggest a layer of pith or skin. The exterior is painted with three bands of pebble glazes (yellow, blue and green) over a dry slip. Pebble glaze is brushed on in a continuous thick layer, but the elastic properties it contains mean that, when it is heated, the glaze fragments and curls up. 'To get the best from a glaze you need to recognise its subtleties and then exploit them. This is what makes a piece sing out, rather than just sit there.'

Single, Double and Triple Heart Peapod, 1998 Maximum 1.70cm Earthenware. Press-moulded and coil-built body with double wall, hand-built handle. Coloured glaze on handle, coloured and pebble glazes on interior and rim, pebble glazes over a dry slip on exterior.

The hearts in these pieces were press-moulded first, then the rim and outer wall were added by coil-building. 'The pods seem to suggest boats or musical instruments. The idea is that the viewer might imagine that the seeds inside the pod were heart-shaped.' (Glaze detail opposite.)

Juicy Heart Sliced Fruit of Your Dreams, 1997-8 Earthenware. Coil-built with double wall. Slips, coloured and pebble glazes.

Love Hearts, the pastel-coloured sherbet sweets, were a source of inspiration for the heart-shaped wells in this group of sliced fruits. As ever, the colour contrasts between the glazes on the three different planes of this vessel – interior, rim and exterior – are carefully chosen for maximum visual effect. The outside is decorated with turquoise glaze over yellow pebble glaze over black slip. (For detail of glaze, see overleaf.)

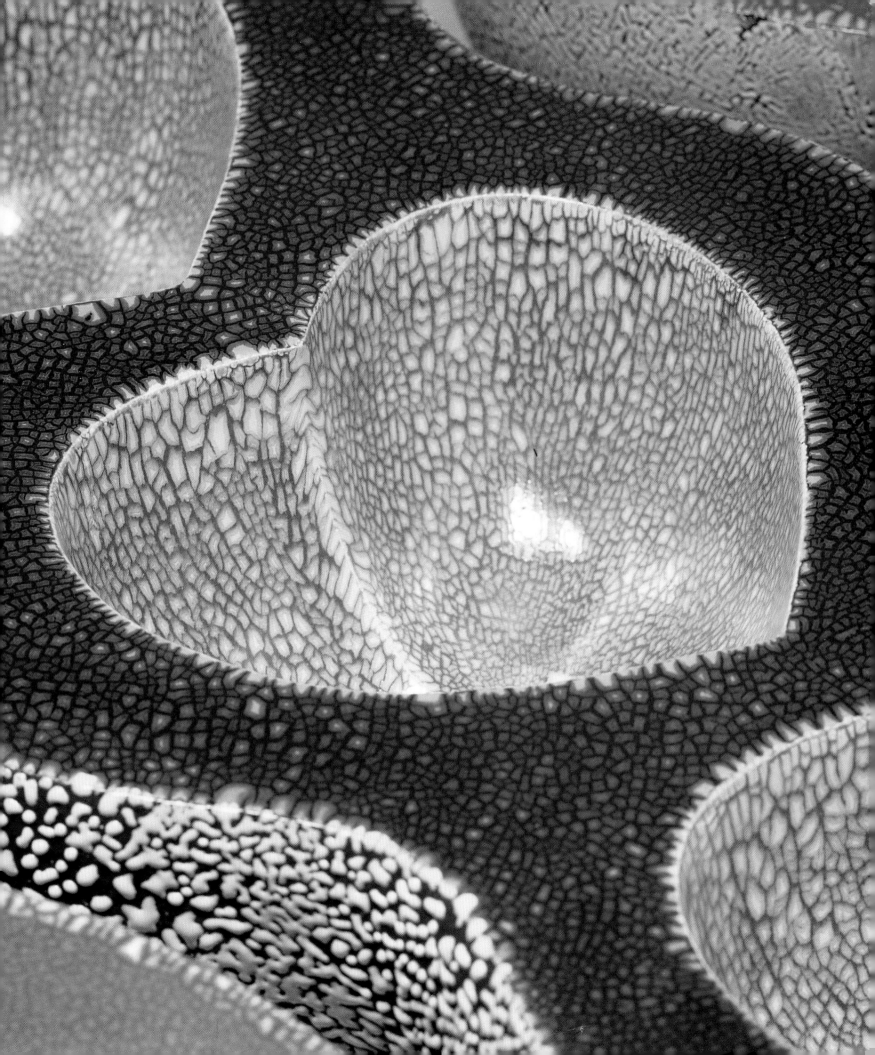

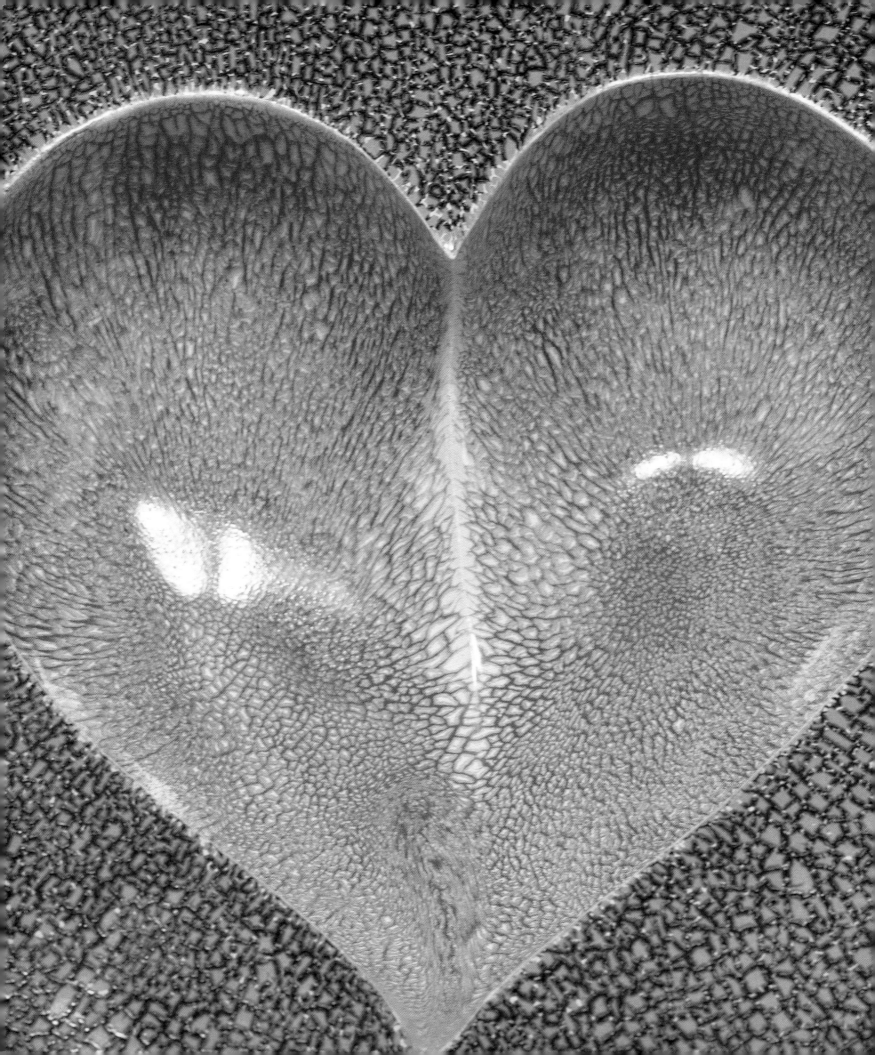

Detail of crystalline glazes
on *Triple Heart Pod, 1998*

(page 89) *Baby Sliced Fruit of Your Dreams, 1995-2000* Various sizes: *8-10cm* Earthenware. Press-moulded, solid. Dry slips, coloured and pebble glazes.

These Baby Sliced Fruits initially served as tests for Kate's pebble glazes, but were subsequently developed as a moderately priced production range at the time of her national touring exhibition *The Allotment*.

The exhibition opened at the Midlands Arts Centre, Birmingham in 1998, and toured to ten venues over the next two years. In keeping with the allotment theme, these pieces were arranged in rows like seedlings, displayed under clear perspex covers resembling cloches. The range consists of seven shapes: sliced pumpkin, lobed nut, avocado, heart, double pea, triple pea and lemon.

Triple Heart Pod, 1998 h.16cm, d.40cm Stoneware. Press-moulded and coil-built with double wall. Crystalline glazes.

'Crystals grow best in pools on horizontal surfaces. My sliced fruit shapes were partly developed for this reason. There's a slight raised lip encircling the rim and around each heart, acting as an invisible barrier to stop the glazes running down the sides of the vessel and into the wells.'

Triple Heart Pod – Love Grows, 1998
l.80cm
Stoneware. Coil-built body with double wall, hand-built handle. Crystalline glazes.
Collection of Los Angeles County Museum (Purchased with funds provided by the Decorative Arts Council)

This piece differs from Kate's other sliced fruits in that the heart-shaped compartments have a flat base. During the glaze firing the vessel tipped to one side, creating sloping pools which echo the arrow-like movement of the piece – a happy accident.

Baby Heart Pod, 1998
h.12cm, d.20cm
Stoneware. Press-moulded
with double wall.
Crystalline glazes.

This medium-sized press-
moulded pod was specially
designed as an affordable
piece to sell during *The
Allotment* exhibition in

1988. Since then around
fifty pieces have been
produced. Although by this
date Kate was aware of how
crystalline glazes behave in
particular circumstances,
the heart-shaped glaze pool
in the well of this pod was
another happy accident –
not something consciously
planned.

Sliced Eye Fruit of Your Dreams, 1991. d.44cm Stoneware. Press-moulded in two parts with double wall, carved on the rim. Crystalline glazes.

This piece was created using the same mould as Sliced Sun Fruit of Your Dreams (see pages 50-51). The rim is carved with an eye instead of a sun, and the glaze pool resembles the eye's pupil. The soft grey-blue glaze colour was produced by combining iron with cobalt.

94

Detail of crystalline glaze pool on *Sliced Eye Fruit of Your Dreams, 1991*

The fleck of turquoise in the centre was the result of an accidental glaze drip falling between two shelves from another pot stacked above this one in the kiln.

Crystalline glazes are
extremely runny at high
temperatures. This detail
illustrates how the glazes
move in response to the
form. Gathering to a tip
at the foot of each segment,
the glazes create feathery
effects reminiscent of
crocus flowers.

Deep Sliced Pumpkin, 1994
h.48cm, d.36cm
Stoneware. Coil-built
with double wall.
Crystalline glazes.

(page 98)
Detail of rim and interior of
Deep Sliced Pumpkin, 1994

The rim of this vessel is
slightly convex, causing
the glazes to trickle down
over the lip. Unusually, the
interior of this double-walled
pot has two distinct tiers –
a well within a well. This,
combined with the ribs
running down inside, affects
the flow and pooling of the
glazes, influencing how the
crystals grow.

(page 99)
Detail of rim and interior
of *Lotus Sliced Fruit, 1994*
h.22cm, d.48cm
Stoneware. Coil-built
with double wall.
Crystalline glazes.

The striking mottled effects
on the wide flat rim of this
piece were produced by
overlaying five different
crystalline glazes in the
one same glaze firing.

Big Slice, 1994
h.27cm, d.56cm
Stoneware. Coil-built
with double skin.
Crystalline glazes.

Big Slice was made at the
same time as Lotus Sliced
Fruit, using the same
technique of multiple glazes
on the rim. The major

difference is the matt finish
of the crystalline glaze on
the outside – an effect Kate
has since been unable to
repeat. The degree of inward
curvature towards the foot
of this vessel means that the
pot has 'lift', even without
the help of a rounded 'belly
button' base.

Fruit Music Woman, 1994
h.26cm, l.66cm, w.30cm
Stoneware. Coil-built body
with double wall, hand-built
hollow handle.
Crystalline glazes.

'Fruit Music Woman was
inspired by buying big
papayas in India, slicing
them in half, and filling

them with fruit for breakfast.
While I was making the
underside, I was thinking
of Salvador Dali's Lip Settee.'
With its flamboyant scroll
handle and crisp ribbed
detailing, Fruit Music
Woman also evokes stringed
instruments, especially lutes,
cellos and violins. Boats also
come to mind.

Heart Walnut, 1998
h.22cm, w.42cm
Stoneware. Coil-built
with double wall.
Crystalline glazes.

'In 1998 I was invited to
make some pots inspired by
objects in Ipswich Museum.
This piece was directly
influenced by a collection of
nuts and seeds gathered by
Professor Henslow, a pioneer
natural historian, on his
travels around the world.
Many of his specimens
were sliced in half, and one
revealed a heart cavity just
like this. The partition wall

has a hole in it connecting
the two cavities, which are
like cavities in a human
heart. When I was finishing
this piece I cut several
cracks in the flat horizontal
rim to suggest a hollow,
rather than a solid mass.
This was quite a challenge,
as I like the apparent solidity
of the thick double-walled
pieces.'

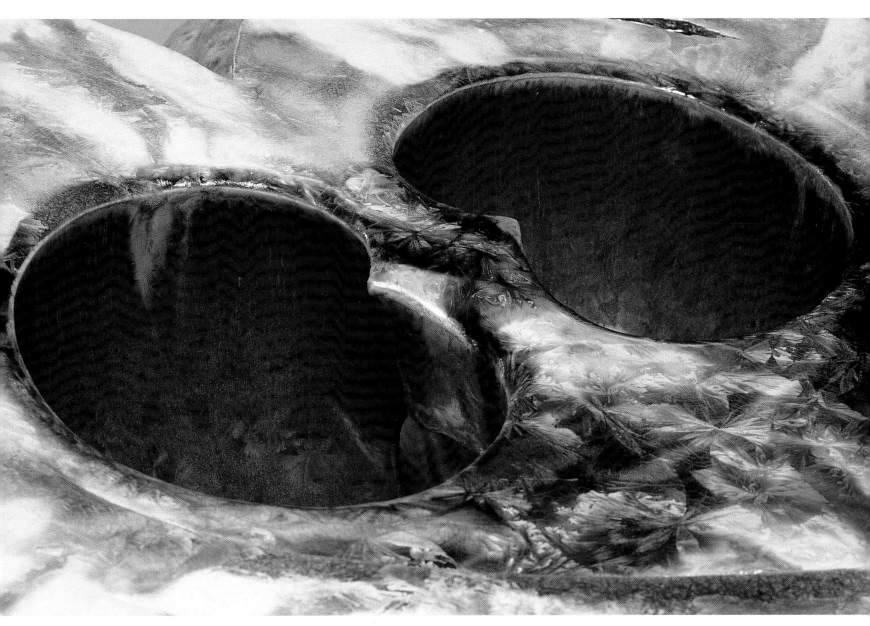

Detail of *Heart Walnut, 1998*

Prince Pine Cone, c.1993
h.18cm
Stoneware. Press-moulded
body, coil-built neck,
hand-built handle.
Crystalline glazes.

Originally dark blue glaze
was applied all over the
exterior of the neck. During
the firing turquoise glaze
has slipped off the rim,
pushing the darker blue
down.

Shell Studded Roll Top Pot,
1993
h.18cm
Stoneware. Press-moulded
body, coil-built neck, applied
press-moulded sprigs.
Crystalline glazes.

'If I have an idea, I often
start three or four pots in
a row so that variations can
follow, keeping one to the
original plan. When they are
finished, usually one sings
out as the better piece. I was
particularly satisfied with
the volume and proportions
of this little pot. The mould
for the sprigs was taken
from a real snail shell.'

Small Honey Bee Pot, 1996
h.42cm
Stoneware. Coil-built,
applied press-moulded
sprigs. Crystalline glazes.

Detail of sprigs and glazes
on neck of *Small Honey
Bee Pot, 1996*

The bee sprig used to
decorate this pot – based
on an old English variety –
was originally modelled
for the bronze fountain in
the Geffrye Museum's herb
garden. (See page 156.)
The honey-coloured streaks
on the neck are intended
to suggest trails of honey
dripping from the bees'
legs, or the path of their
flight. Up to four glazes
were dabbed on in different
layers (for the same firing)
to create these unrepeatable
effects.

Like Bees to a Honey Pot,
1996
h.68cm, d.38cm
Stoneware. Wheel-thrown
body, coil-built neck,
hand-built rim, applied
press-moulded sprigs.
Crystalline glazes.

Kate's pots often have
an inner life, and she
frequently applies sprigs
or glazes on the interior
that tempt people to look
inside. The bees on this vase
become less dense as they
fly out from inside the belly
of the pot.

Giant Queen Tea Pot, 1998
h.50cm, w.82cm
Stoneware. Coil-built body,
hand-built spout, handle
and knob. Applied press-
moulded, impressed and
hand-modelled sprigs.
Crystalline glazes.
Collection of Norwich Castle
Museum

This is the sister piece to
the giant teapot created
to sit on top of the clock
commissioned for the
Bentalls Shopping Centre
at Kingston-on-Thames
(see pages 150-51), which
explains why it is oval in
aerial view. Produced as a
'reserve' in case of accidents

during the firing of the
commissioned piece, Giant
Queen Tea Pot is intended
to embody the essence of the
classic 'Brown Betty' teapot,
celebrating the great British
tradition of sitting down
with family and friends to
enjoy a refreshing cup of
tea. The spout and handle

were initially carved from
solid clay, then hollowed out.
Several full-size variants
were modelled originally,
so that Kate could decide
which worked best in
relation to the body, their
scale and profile being
crucial to the success of
the vessel as a whole.

Detail of *sprigs on Giant Queen Tea Pot, 1998*

Sprigging is a key element in Kate's decorative repertoire, and her technique of producing these low-relief motifs is distinctive. The original clay sprig used to create a plaster mould is modelled in the desired shape and contours, but without fine details. Press-moulded sprigs produced from this mould are joined to the wetted and scratched main body. Only then are fine details added using a tool pressed through cling film. This technique ensures that each sprig has individuality, making them look fresh and crisp. Working on the sprig after it has been applied also helps to bond it to the piece. The sprigged motifs on Giant Queen Tea Pot represent Kate's personal family of symbols. Pumpkins for fertility, gourds for fecundity, pineapples for prosperity and hospitality, leaves and flowers for nature, bees for industry, jugs for sharing. Various other insects are hidden inside the pot, including a beetle crawling inside the spout. This teapot took pride of place in *The Allotment* exhibition, where it served as the symbolic 'watering can' for the fruit and vegetables in the show. It has since been acquired by Norwich Castle Museum, renowned for their collection of historic British teapots.

Stamen and Studded Vase, c.1998
h.72cm, d.43cm
Stoneware. Wheel-thrown body, coil-built neck. Press-moulded applied bulbs on body, applied hand-modelled surface decoration on neck. Crystalline glazes.

Created in response to the Victorian natural history collections at Ipswich Museum, this idiosyncratic tall vase was inspired by Professor Henslow's drawings and wall charts, recording plants seen on his global expeditions. The press-moulded studs are the same as those on Kate's Tutti Frutti pots, each hollow spike being created in a plaster mould originally cast from a pointed light bulb. 'I was trying to suggest stamens erupting from a prickly tropical seed.'

*Mother and Daughter, 1988
Mother: h.68cm; Daughter:
h.53cm*
Earthenware. Coil-built.
Matt rutile glaze and multi-
coloured 'Snowfall' glazes.

A good designer often has a
natural sense of proportion
which, Kate feels, will be
similar to the Golden
Section, a mathematical
pattern reflected in nature.

Kate normally determines
the scale of her pieces
instinctively, but these pots
– produced as an exercise
in applying the laws of the
Golden Section – were
carefully made to precise
measurements using
callipers. The Golden Section
dictates both their overall
width and height, as well
as the position and diameter
of their waists and necks.

The dimensions of the
mother and daughter
therefore relate
mathematically to each
other, and their contrasting
smooth and textured
glazes are also intended
to be complementary. Coil-
building the ribbed flared
necks of these large pieces
proved particularly difficult.

Popping Seed Jug, 1998
h.32cm
Stoneware. Press-moulded
body and handle, applied
hand-modelled surface
decoration.
Crystalline glazes.

The essence of the pine cone
has proved more elusive to
pin down than that of the
pineapple. This quilted pot
marked Kate's third attempt
to clothe a vessel in a pine
cone-type jacket.
(See page 104.)

Brother and Sister Crystal
Seed Head Vases, 2000
Maximum h.18cm
Stoneware. Press-moulded
body, press-moulded applied
bulbs. Crystalline glazes.

'I was curious to see what
the Tutti Frutti pots would
look like with crystalline
glazes. Normally I cloak
them with pebble glazes,
which are thick and opaque
like custard. The crystalline
glazes are the opposite, and
the effect is quite different.'

Small Studded Seed Head Vase, 2001
h.14cm
Stoneware. Press-moulded body, press-moulded applied bulbs. Crystalline glazes.

Pots with applied decoration of this kind are extremely time-consuming to make. Kate relies heavily on her helpers to press-mould the constituent parts for these pieces, which she then applies. This is one of the jobs on which her apprentices cut their teeth when they first come to work for her in the studio. 'If I didn't have my wonderful apprentices or assistant, I don't think I would be making such labour-intensive pieces. Circumstances like this inevitably influence your work. I really enjoy the labour intensiveness of building these pieces. To spend a whole day applying the bulbs is one of my favourite tasks. Like embroidery or needlepoint, the activity is repetitive but not mindless. Concentration has to be maintained to do the job properly. At the same time it's very relaxing; the rhythm is absorbing. I hope this shows in the finished piece.'

Small Garlic Bud Vase, 2001
h.14cm
Stoneware. Press-moulded
body, applied hand-modelled
pinch pot cloves.
Crystalline glazes.

Bursting Garlic Bud Bottle, 2001
h.38cm
Stoneware. Press-moulded body, applied hand-modelled pinch pots.
Crystalline glazes.

'The applied decoration on this pot was inspired by a garlic flower that had gone to seed. Whereas on the Tutti Frutti pieces the studs are press-moulded, here each segment is a hollow pinch pot modelled by hand, then built on to the surface. I wanted to see the difference between component parts made freehand, and those pressed in moulds. The subtle shape of the pot was inspired by the trunks of some ancient tree ferns I saw in New Zealand, particularly the sections of the trunk where the ferns had come away. It also recalls the forms of the Staffordshire celery jars I collect.'

Detail of bulbs on *Bursting Garlic Bud Bottle, 2001*

This close-up reveals of the delicacy of the hand-modelling on each segment. The brown tinges in the honey-coloured glazes, suggesting discolouration, are another wonderfully subtle detail.

Firework Splash, 2001
h.15cm
Stoneware. Press-moulded body, applied hand-modelled fingers. Crystalline glazes.

Because the fingers on this pot are pointing downwards, they look like fireworks exploding in the sky. Streaked glazes on the neck accentuate these starburst effects.

Detail of fingers on *Firework Splash, 2001*

A ridged bead was pressed into the holes cut into the body before the fingers were inserted on this piece, hence the 'pinking' around the base of each prong.

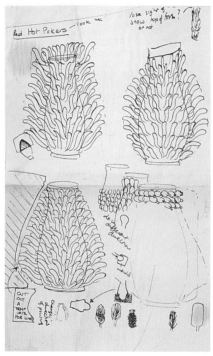

Drawings for *Red Hot Poker* series

The First Red Hot Poker – But not Red, 2001
h.18cm
Stoneware. Press-moulded body, applied hand-modelled fingers. Crystalline glazes.

As its title suggests, this piece (and the ensuing group) was inspired by red hot pokers, a strangely exotic yet commonplace country garden flower. Each tapering finger was hand-modelled by rolling and bending into shape. When stiff enough, the fingers were pushed through holes pierced in the body, which were then plugged from the inside. After being fired, the fingers make a tinkling percussion sound.

Detail of *Tutti Frutti Red Hot Poker*, 2001

Tutti Frutti Red Hot Poker, 2001
h.14cm
Earthenware. Press-moulded body, applied hand-modelled fingers. Coloured and pebble glazes.

This piece was made using the same techniques as the Crystalline Hot Pokers, but pebble glazes completely transform its character. Each finger has a double-thick layer of rosso red glaze, twice-fired, and then the third firing combines rosso red glaze with yellow and pink pebble glazes. Because the fingers are so close together, painting on the glazes takes considerable patience and dexterity. It took five hours to paint on the pebble glaze layer which was the fourth glaze firing in the kiln.

*Multi-coloured Tutti Frutti
Berry, 2001*
h.24cm
Earthenware. Press-moulded
body, coil-built neck, hand-
built leaves, press-moulded
and manipulated applied
balls. Coloured and pebble
glazes.

The first time Kate used
light bulbs to make moulds
was for her Tutti Frutti
Bumper Car Jugs. Since
then she has built up quite
a collection – including a
group of vintage bulbs given
to her by an enthusiast in an
electrical shop – which she
now regularly uses to create
one- or two-part plaster
moulds. The press-moulded
balls on this pot are of two
different sizes, and she has
used them to play with the
dynamics of decoration and
scale. Four different glaze
firings were needed to create
the effects on this piece:
three firings to get the base
glaze adequately thick and
even, and then one final
firing for the pebble glazes,
painted on in three
separate layers.

Nuts and Berries
Exhibition at Dover Street
Gallery, London, May-June
2000

'This row of pots was
intended to evoke the idea
of a line of people in a bus
queue. Whether young or
old, male or female, each
person / pot has their own
idiosyncratic characteristics.
The baby berry at the end
is small enough to sit in
the palm of your hand.'

*The First Blackberry, 2000
h.26cm*
Stoneware. Press-moulded
body, coil-built neck, hand-
built leaves, press-moulded
and manipulated applied
balls. Crystalline glazes.

'This was the first in a
series of pots made for the
exhibition *Nuts and Berries*,
held at the Dover Street
Gallery in 2000, inspired
by picking blackberries in
the autumn, and thinking
how completely beautiful
each one is. Blackberries
hold red juice inside a blue-
black skin, so the logical
thing to do when trying to
replicate this effect with
glaze is to apply two layers
of different coloured glazes.
Here I used midnight blue
over dark aubergine. Both
glazes were given a separate
firing, although with
crystalline glazes this can
be problematic because so
much glaze runs off the pot.'

Naughty Boy Blackberry,
2000, h.18cm
Stoneware. Press-moulded
body, coil-built neck, hand-
built leaves, press-moulded
and manipulated applied
balls. Crystalline glazes.

One ball on this blackberry
pot has been deliberately left
green, simulating a quirk
in nature.

Big Bold Blackberry Jug,
2000
h.32cm
Stoneware. Press-moulded
body, coil-built neck, hand-
built leaves, press-moulded
and manipulated applied
balls. Crystalline glazes.

The balls on this jug were
decorated with the same
dual-layer glaze combination
as the two previous pieces,
but on each pot the colours
have come out quite
differently because there are
so many variables within the
crystalline glazing process.

Detail of *The Two Aunties,
2000*
h.28cm
Stoneware. Press-moulded
body, coil-built neck, hand-
built leaves, press-moulded
and manipulated applied
balls. Crystalline glazes.

This close-up highlights the
textural and tonal variety of
the glazes with which Kate
experimented in this series.

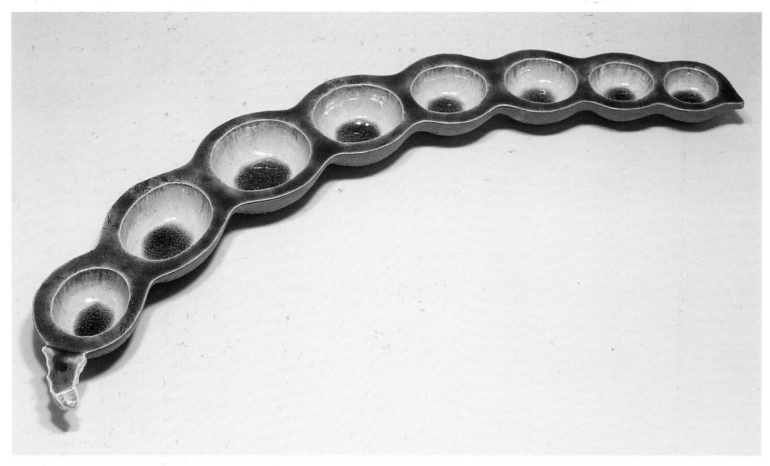

Sri Lankan Long Seed Pod, 2001
82cm
Stoneware. Hand-built, solid. Coloured slip and crystalline glazes.

Sri Lankan Long Seed Pod reflects Kate's on-going search for interesting new ceramic forms inspired by fruit, vegetables, pods, nuts and seeds from around the world. 'This piece was inspired by a huge bean I brought back from Sri Lanka. Eight pinch pots of diminishing sizes were laid upside down, then bridged together from the back. To prevent this extra-long thin shape from breaking during drying and handling, a bespoke cradle was created to support it, which was used right through the entire making and firing process.'

*Mad Meissen Brussels
Sprouts Vase, 1999
h.47cm*
Stoneware. Press-moulded
body, press-moulded applied
bulbs. Crystalline glaze.

The term Mad Meissen
refers to the so-called
Schneeballen vases produced
by the Meissen porcelain
factory. In these pieces a
conventional vase was
transformed through the
addition of giant snowball-
like extrusions, themselves
coated with a blanket of tiny
flower heads. Kate found
the extravagant over-the-
top nature of these vases
hilarious. The idea of
dressing up an ordinary
vessel by adding multiple
layers of relief decoration
also had parallels with her
own work. Mad Meissen
Brussels Sprouts Vase
was her first venture into
this genre, which she
subsequently explored
through a series of
variations on a theme.
'The two-part moulds for
the appendages were taken
from a variety of light bulbs.
Each ball is separately press-
moulded, then meticulously
hand-worked to remove the
seams. Crystalline glazes
are completely unforgiving
of blemishes on the surface
of the clay – any fault is
magnified, and cracks are
made bigger by the sheer
clarity of the glaze – so
everything has to be
perfectly made and joined,
which takes hours of
patient, careful work.'

Brussels Sprouts Bottle,
2000
h.38cm
Stoneware. Press-moulded
body, press-moulded applied
bulbs. Crystalline glazes.

The immediate inspiration
for this pot was a
magnificent brussels
sprouts stem presented to
Kate by some friends. The
sprout-like quality of the
appendages is emphasised
by the yellowy-green glazes.
'The stalk was thick and
chunky, and the sprouts
protruded in a rhythmic
pattern reminiscent of
pineapples and pine cones.'

Princess Leia Mad Meissen Bottles, 2000
h.38cm
Stoneware. Press-moulded body, sprigged bobbles on press-moulded applied bulbs. Crystalline glazes.

Princess Leia is a character in the film *Star Wars* who wore her hair in two coiled buns on the side of her head.

'These two appendages were very heavy and the point of contact between the ball and the body was very small, so they had to be joined to the vessel very carefully to prevent them cracking or bending downwards. I wasn't sure that these pieces would survive the high temperature firing.'

Atomic Bowl, 2001
h.26cm, w.54cm
Stoneware. Coil-built body,
sprigged bobbles on press-
moulded applied bulbs.
Crystalline glazes.

'My recent work has become
more abstract, and seems to
have taken on microscopic
and atomic qualities. This
piece brings to mind ball
and spoke atomic models,
and reminds me of the space
station fantasies my brother
used to tell me as a child.'

Detail of crystals on interior
of *Atomic Bowl, 2001*

'The single large cluster of
crystals in the well of this
bowl came as a complete
surprise. Measuring about
12cm across, it looks like a
galaxy in space.'

A group of *Baby Lady Vases, 2002.* For the Geffrye Museum show. *h.18cm each piece* Stoneware. Press-moulded body, sprigged and applied balls.

Top left –
Cactus Atomic Lady Vase
Top right –
Pom Pom Lady Vase
Bottom left –
Pom Pom Lady Vase
Bottom right –
Necklaced Lady Vase

The five examples shown here are part of an experiment to see how different surface treatments can affect a single form. Thirty 'lady vases' were pressed from a two-piece plaster mould. Each one's surface was decorated in a different way. It is interesting to see that although the vase on the bottom right is the same basic form as the one on the bottom left, the neck and shape on the right seem more dynamic and the body taller.

*Atomic Sweep Baby Vase,
2002*
h.18cm
Stoneware. Press-moulded
body, sprigged press-
moulded applied bulbs.
Crystalline glazes.

*Mrs Maddest Meissen,
1999-2000*
h.66cm
Stoneware. Coil-built body,
sprigged bobbles on press-
moulded applied bulbs.
Crystalline glazes.

'This pot was fired upside
down on a tower of kiln
props so that the glaze drips
would point upwards; it's all
about the essence of growth,
the "life force". This was a
huge risk with a piece this
size and weight, which
contains 25 kilograms of
clay, and measures over half
a metre, but T Material is
a wonderful clay body and,
as usual, withstood these
demands. Most other clays
would bend or crack at such
high temperatures on such
a large piece.'

Mr Maddest Meissen,
1999-2000
h.66cm
Stoneware. Coil-built body,
sprigged bobbles on press-
moulded applied bulbs.
Crystalline glazes.

'The idea of this piece was
to make it seem as if the
clay "bubbles" or balls are
floating in mid air – losing
track of the central form.'

Commissions

Why make large-scale works?

It has been my long-term ambition to be a maker of great big pots – so huge, in fact, that it was logical to turn to the public and commercial sectors for placing them. My aim is to produce work for a wide audience. Higher-priced 'one of a kind' pieces are purchased by museums and collectors, while studio-produced editions cater for a middle range. When I left college I thought that collaborating with industry was the way to make my work widely affordable and reach the general public. In fact, as it turned out, it has been through large-scale works for the public sector that I have reached a wider audience.

In 1989 I had a serious illness, and experienced at first hand the benefits of a superb hospital arts project at Homerton Hospital in Hackney, London. Since then I have particularly enjoyed placing work in hospitals (including Homerton). The optimistic symbolism that I use is particularly appropriate in hospitals. I have also been commissioned to create indoor and outdoor works for parks, museums, shopping centres and office foyers.

Handling commissions

Having recognised that I wanted to place work in the public sector, I turned to the commissions section of *Artists Newsletter* (now *AN Magazine For Artists*). I also registered with various arts development agencies, some of which were listed in *AN*. Attending conferences and networking proved useful, and

I also wrote to architects whose work I admired. I have strong views about the benefits of placing ceramics in the public domain. Used correctly, this radiant, low maintenance material can be remarkably durable. One only has to look at the fabulous terracotta reliefs on the Natural History Museum in London, Gaudi's work in Barcelona and the many richly tiled British public houses and London Underground stations, to appreciate the versatility of the medium and how well ceramics lasts the test of time. Having registered your interest in being considered for a commission, the standard procedure is for a few short-listed artists to be invited to produce proposal ideas from a written brief. It is normal to expect a proposal fee, as it takes a lot of time and careful thought to formulate a written proposal. The proposal acts as a vehicle for illustrating your concept, and demonstrating your awareness of the practicalities of producing large-scale work. Key points to address in a proposal include:

Basic materials
• Extra components and special fixtures (e.g. water pumps, clock mechanisms), and the additional professional services required to plan and install
• Installation specifications (e.g. bonding materials for mounting)
• Safety aspects
• Durability
• Life expectancy of materials and components
• On-going maintenance

requirements after installation
• Sensitivity to specific surroundings
• Relevance to the community
• Delivery
• Schedule of payment

Costing a commission is particularly difficult, and it is easy to underestimate the amount of time involved. In my experience it takes as much time to organise a project as to make the actual piece. My advice for calculating a realistic fee is to take your initial figure, then double it. Often the budget is fixed in the brief, so your proposal needs to be tailored within these constraints. Although the proposal document does not need to be lavishly produced, it must be clear, accurate and concise. This is important because it tells the client what you will be like to work with. I take photos on site visits and incorporate them in my proposal, alongside drawings. My proposal illustrations are fairly rough and are not presented as technical drawings, but these sketches are supported by a typed document demonstrating a thorough awareness of the scale and demands of the project, along with a CV and images of other work.

It is important to retain a degree of flexibility when presenting your proposed ideas, as a certain amount of creative freedom is essential to produce good work. Although deadlines are a key element of any project, a flexible completion date is preferable as it is difficult to estimate precisely how long it

will take to complete a large piece, and it generally takes twice as long as you think. If the piece has a projected lifespan of twenty years, it is foolish to rush a commission and risk the quality of the finished work with a tight deadline.

In my experience undertaking a public project is 5% inspiration and 95% perspiration. Tenacity is the name of the game. Before embarking on a project, all parties need to agree a clear method of communication – including yourself, the commissioning agent and /or the client. Once the go ahead and initial payment have been received, then the real work begins. Faced with the reality of a daunting project, it is best to approach it one step at a time. Once the momentum has been generated, problem solving becomes part of the challenge. Site preparation and careful attention to installation details are both extremely important. If a beautiful piece is installed in a badly prepared site or mounted on an ugly plinth, all your fine work is wasted. In the end job satisfaction overrides the strenuous effort of working on a large scale.

Hackney Marshes Commission

Initial concept drawing.

Fish *in situ* in the disused drinking water filter beds.

Rise and Shine Magic Fish, 1990-1991

A set of fish sculptures for Lea Valley Park, Hackney Marshes Nature Reserve, East London. Commissioned by Lea Valley Public Art, project-managed by The Public Art Development Trust. Various heights: *100-112cm.*
Stoneware. Coil-built, hand-built and carved. Crystalline glazes.

The sculptures, installed in the disused drinking water filter beds at Hackney Marshes, take the form of fish breaking the surface of the water. The brief was to educate and entertain visitors at this urban nature reserve, so I chose to model English freshwater fish – carp, pike and rudd. Fish heads, backs and tails are mounted on hardwood railway sleepers, bolted together under the water. One newspaper commented that it looked as if the fishes were so choked by the polluted waters in London that they were gasping for breath. However, my idea was to suggest them playing joyously in the water. Community and education programmes ran alongside the making and installation of the fish. (See p.140 for project *in situ*.)

Glazed pieces in the studio after firing.

Homerton Hospital Commission

Life Pours Forth, 1990-91
A courtyard fountain
for Homerton Hospital,
Hackney, London.
Commissioned by
Homerton Hospital
Arts Committee, project-
managed by The Public
Art Development Trust.
h.104cm
Earthenware. Coil-built,
applied sprigs. Coloured
glazes.

The fountain takes the
form of a large jug with
fish spiralling up around
its body, which constantly
pours water into a giant
bowl. The tank and pump
are buried beneath the
ground.
Symbolism:
A fish rising is a symbol
of life improving.
The colour blue is calming.
A large pot is a symbol of
strength and stability.
A jug is a symbol of sharing
and friendship.
A fountain symbolises life
regenerating.

Painting on the coloured
earthenware glazes.

Fountain *in situ* in
courtyard at Homerton
Hospital.

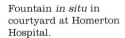

Detail of large press-
moulded sprigged fishes
and coloured glazes.

Castle Park Drinking Fountain Commission

Drinking Fountain, 1993-4
Bronze drinking water fountain in Castle Park, Bristol. Commissioned by Bristol City Council, project-managed by Lesley Greene.
h.106cm, w.100cm
Bronze cast from coil-built, hand-built and hand-modelled biscuit-fired ceramic master.

The fountain is located at the start of the Sustrans Bristol-to-Bath Cycle Path. Two fish at the top squirt water when the eye of a fish on the side is pressed. My original proposal of a doggy drinking moat around the base was changed, as the Council did not want to encourage dogs in this central city park.

Bronze drinking fountain *in situ* at Castle Park.

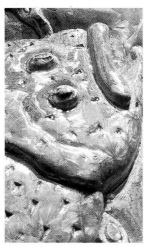

Ceramic original, re-fired with crystalline glaze. *Collection of Bristol City Museums and Galleries.*

Biscuit-fired pot emerging from the trolley kiln.

146

The design incorporates references to Bristol's maritime heritage and the history of Castle Park, alluding both to the shape of a cog merchant ship, and the original castle with a double entrance. Other imagery includes tobacco leaves, and fish from the North Sea (fished from Bristol since the 15th century). Saxon coins indicate the year the piece was made. It was difficult to know how to allude to the slave trade with sensitivity. I chose to do this by incorporating a winged face modelled from a slave's grave in a Bristol cemetery.

Because of the risk of vandalism, the piece was cast in bronze from a biscuit-fired clay master. The piece was transported to the Pangolin Foundry at Stroud, where a mould was taken, from which a lost wax bronze cast was made, and then patinated. Afterwards I collected the bisque, re-fired it to burn away any dirt, then fired it again with a crystalline glaze. The ceramic piece was donated to Bristol City Museum and Art Gallery. It is very interesting to see a piece cast into bronze, the main difference to me being that the bronze absorbs light, whereas the ceramic version radiates it.

I also ran a school project alongside this commission. A firm of brickmakers, Ibstock Ltd., supplied raw clay soft bricks. School children, having learnt about the history of the park, made plaster stamps, which they pressed into the bricks. These were then fired by Ibstock, and installed around the base of the piece.

Royal Devon & Exeter Hospital Commission

Swim Fishes Swim, 1996, and *Undersea Garden, 2001*
Two groups of marine sculptures for a courtyard project at the Children's Oncology Ward, Royal Devon & Exeter Hospital, Wonford Site, Barrack Road, Exeter. Commissioned by Exeter Healthcare Arts.
Fountain: 3.32cm, w.120cm.
Seahorse: h.50cm.
Shells: d.25cm-34cm
Earthenware. Press-moulded, sprigged and hand-built. Coloured glazes, multiple glaze-fired.

These commissions were undertaken in two separate stages, five years apart. Initially I was invited to 'do something' with a rather ugly fountain that had been built in the hospital courtyard. I used ready-made blue tiles to clad the tank. Hand-built, sprigged and press-moulded fish and sea creatures of various sizes were then bonded into place on top, resulting in a complete transformation.

Above, proposal illustrations. Below, views of the fish tank fountain

Five years later I was invited to add to the scheme by creating a series of free-standing sculptures for the surrounding courtyard garden. I made a group of press-moulded and hand-built shells, starfish and seahorses, which are hidden amongst the foliage, while three shoals of fish swim over the bushes, mounted on metal rods. I also made two large fish seats and coral stools for the children to sit on. The courtyard is a waiting area for children who may visit the hospital for treatment on a regular basis. The idea is that they can fill their time by hunting for the fifty or so hidden sea creatures.

Bentalls Shopping Centre Commission

Time for Tea Teapot Clock, 1998
Double-sided clock with a teapot on the top that steams every hour, Bentalls Shopping Centre, Kingston-upon-Thames, Surrey. Whole Clock project managed by Brookbrae Ltd.
Teapot: h.50cm, w.82cm.
Clock face: d.3m. Mounted on a column 12m above the ground.
Teapot: Stoneware. Coil-built and hand-built. Crystalline glazes. Clock face: Stoneware hour markers co-designed and modelled by Jola Spytkowska, mounted on steel and aluminium.

Twenty-four individually modelled hour markers are mounted on the two faces of the double-sided clock. They combine a mixture of my personal symbols, such as jugs and pineapples, with images of food, intended to encourage shoppers to visit the food hall (part of the client's brief). The huge teapot on top, which spouts steam every hour, provides a regular reminder that it is time for a cup of tea. (For a close-up of a similar teapot, see Giant Queen Tea Pot, pages 108-9.)

Photomontage showing the clock being installed.

Queen Pineapple Commission

Queen Pineapple, 1995
Commissioned by
Manchester City Art
Galleries.
Stoneware. Coil-built,
applied hand-built and
hand-modelled surface
relief decoration.
Crystalline glazes.
h.108cm, w.87cm.

In 1994 I held a solo show
at Manchester City Art
Galleries called Fruits of
the Earth and Sea. This
prompted the Galleries
to commission a major
piece for their collection,
originally installed in
their café.

Hollow press-moulded
pyramid-shaped segments
are applied to the body, and
modelled into the correct
shape on the pot. Starting
from the shoulder, working
around the body in circles,
each diamond segment is
individually hand-modelled
without the use of tools.

With a large commission,
as a safeguard against
accidents, I start by making
two pieces. This also gives
me a degree of freedom to
choose which is the most
appropriate shape to follow
through. The second piece
is held in reserve to develop
in a different way at a later
date, if all goes well. The pot
on the right became Queen
Pineapple; the pot on the
left later became an
Artichoke Studded Pot .Each
piece weighs approximately
a quarter of a ton. The two
small pots on the floor in the
foreground – Choir Boy and
Choir Girl Pineapples
(see pages 44-5) – show
the proposed idea on a
small scale.

The first hand-built leaf is applied to the neck. The tip is held in position until it stiffens enough to hold its shape.

Applying the third leaf to the neck.

Applying the second tier of leaves to the neck.

Dry raw clay *Queen Pineapple* in the studio before biscuit firing. Photographs were taken at this stage in case the piece exploded in the kiln. Even though each hollow diamond segment was created with a breather hole into the core of the pot, with so much squeezing and pushing of the clay I was worried that air might have got trapped, causing a section to blow out. I reckoned that there was a one-in-six chance of losing this complex piece after four months' work. At this stage the piece was dry and as delicate as a rich tea biscuit. The leaves were particularly fragile. It was a stressful moment when, under my instruction, four strong men, huffing and puffing, lifted this piece, built on its heavy kiln shelf, onto the kiln trolley.

Crystalline-glazed Queen Pineapple sitting on a trolley in the studio, having shrunk 12% during its two firings.

Detail of raw pot. The plasticity of the clay is particularly noticeable here, reflecting the fact that only fingers were used as tools to push and smear the pineapple flesh into shape.

Interior, showing the holes cut in the vessel wall behind each segment to prevent them exploding. Streaks of glaze can be seen running down the inside of the neck and body, with a deep pool of crystals at the bottom. It is interesting that the holes down the sides resemble the way a pineapple looks when it has been peeled, while the huge golden strands of crystals in the base look like pineapple flesh.

Geffrye Museum Herb Garden Commission

Herb Garden Fountain, 1995
Bronze fountain for Herb Garden at the Geffrye Museum, London. Commissioned by the Geffrye Museum, sponsored by Gerrard House.
h.92cm
Bronze cast from coil-built and hand-modelled biscuit-fired ceramic master.

The vase-shaped fountain, installed in the centre of the Herb Garden, magically brims with water, which trickles over the rim into the pool below. The decoration depicts old English bees amongst traditional scented flowers and herbs – honeysuckle, sage, cranesbill and lavender. After the bronze cast had been taken, the master was earthenware glazed and the pot was given to the Geffrye Museum by the sponsors. Bronze was used because of the risk of vandalism; otherwise clay would have been chosen.

Patinating the bronze vessel.

Detail of honeysuckle and bee on the bronze vessel.

Fountain *in situ* in the Herb Garden at the Geffrye Museum.

Greenwich Park Herb Garden Commission

Millennium Fountain, 2000
Bronze artichoke pot
fountain for the Herb Garden
at Greenwich Park.
Commissioned by the
Friends of Greenwich Park.
h.1m
Bronze cast from coil-built
and hand-modelled biscuit-
fired ceramic master.

Mounted on a plinth, the
artichoke pot brims over
with water into the pond
below. Commissioned to
celebrate the new
Millennium, the artichoke
symbolises tenacity, the
large pot symbolises
strength and stability, and
the fountain symbolises
regeneration.

Old Bailey
Office Entrance Area
Commission

Mother and Daughter Pots of Symbols, 2001
Two large vessels commissioned by the Old Bailey Consortium, City of London.
h.120cm
Stoneware. Coil-built, applied sprigs, hand-carved and hand-modelled surface relief decoration, incised inscriptions inside neck. Crystalline glazes.

Both pots are the same size but decorated on a different scale. The mother pot is adorned with small sprigged symbols arranged in a regular pattern, indicating that she is more mature and worldly wise. The daughter pot carries similar images, but magnified onto a giant scale, erupting from the foot ring, dynamic and spring fresh. The two pots are also differentiated by their glazes: the mother's age is denoted by the use of softer and more mottled colours; the daughter's youth is suggested by larger patches of brighter colours. The mother is the 'teacher', so the inscription on the inside of her neck explains the symbolism that both she and her daughter carry.

Adding a thick hand-rolled coil to build up the pot.

Hand-modelling with soft clay on the scoured surface of the daughter.

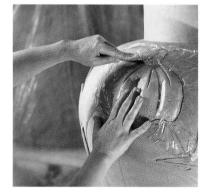

Smoothing the hand-modelled relief decoration through a layer of cling film on the daughter.

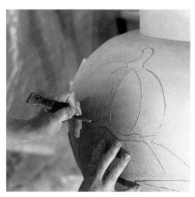

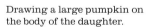

Drawing a large pumpkin on the body of the daughter.

Modelling relief decoration on the daughter pot.

Detail of sprigs on Mother Pot of Symbols.

Mother and Daughter Pots of Symbols, with daughter in the foreground.

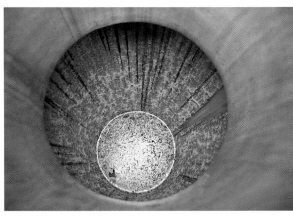

Interior of Daughter Pot of Symbols showing pool of crystalline glaze in well.

Scarlet (Kate's 4 year-old daughter) inside Mother Pot of Symbols.

Interior of Mother Pot of Symbols showing incised inscription around neck.

drink its juice and have

a Gourd a symbol of

of sharing — a bee

Flower opening symbolises

succe...

longevit...

of hard work

symbolises

develop...

Ceramic Rooms
Geffrye Museum Exhibition

Ceramic Rooms – At Home with Kate Malone and Edmund de Waal, The
Geffrye Museum, London, 24 September 2002 – 19 January 2003.
Stoneware and earthenware room, measuring 3.7m x 5m.

Kate and her assistant Michelle Aitken worked on this project for the best part
of a year between September 2001 and September 2002.

The following is taken from texts written by Kate for the exhibition:
'This show is fun, great fun, though also rather serious. As usual I jumped into
a project with gusto then realised that I had taken rather a big bite. This is hard
work, stretching, really exciting, just the way I like it. The Geffrye Museum had
the idea of doing something other than the usual putting of pots onto plinths to
exhibit work. Rather daunted by the size of the exhibition space at the Geffrye,
and wanting to develop my ceramic understanding, I suggested that we bring
the wonderful Edmund de Waal into the exhibition – my ceramic opposite. As
the Geffrye Museum is composed of a series of rooms showing the urban
domestic English living room, the idea of two different rooms evolved in our
minds, an experiment to show different ideals in clay minimalism and
maximalism.

I feel rather responsible as I am waving the flag for maximalism, for the
decorative and the decorated. My aim is to be ebullient and joyous, to show my
love for clay and glazing, and for the magic of the life force. I aim to do this
with a sense of decorative clarity, not too mad, but slightly mad, not tight, but
contained. I rely on instinct, on the subconscious, at the same time selecting
and applying knowledge and a vocabulary which has evolved over 30 years of
working with clay and studying nature. As usual I want to do everything (and
can't). As usual this is an evolution – the room is growing. I wish I had another
year to work on it.

As separate pieces for the room are made, they influence the next ones, the
balance of colour, complexity, scale or quantity of each element. I have had an
overall plan for the room to be very strongly symbolic, optimistic and uplifting.
I did not have an exact finished vision. I have considered clay being used for
living in two ways. Firstly, as interior architecture integral to the room:
fireplace, door furniture, light, patterned walls, floor, seating, skirting board,
small shelves and alcoves. Secondly I have considered the living room as a
place where people display their collections. On the shelf that extends high
around the room is a collection of pots that are all the exactly same base
shape, each wearing a different 'coat' of hand decorated surface. A bit like a
preoccupation of collecting things that are similar but different, seeing things in
repeat, in quantity, in lines. This high shelf is an echo of a picture rail that once
might have displayed a line of collected plates in a middle class English home.

My aim has been to make a room to be used for indulgence, for special

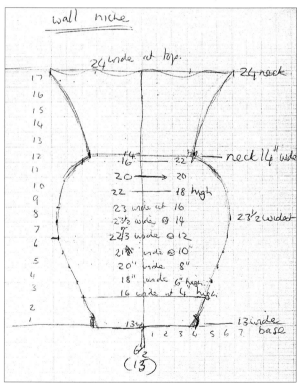

Above, one of the first idea
sketches for the room.
Below, measurements for
making the half pot concave
alcoves either side of the
fireplace.

Above, *The Dream Daisy Chain* light with ceiling leaves and bee. Totally hand built in 4 sections, this up-lights the ceiling and has fibre optic star lights that glisten like drops of pollen on the stamens. A colour wheel at the fibre optic light source makes the lights ripple with changing colours.
Below, *Pumpkin Pouffe*. Press-moulded, crystalline glazed stoneware. Limited edition of 20.

moments and occasions: relaxing, reading, sitting beside the fire thinking (or not thinking at all), meditating, talking, kissing, planning, drinking tea and toasting marshmallows.Thank you very much for this stimulating invitation to work. I love the Geffrye, it is a diamond that shines in the East End of London, please may I now build you a folly in your gardens.'

The following is taken from an article written by Lesley Jackson for the magazine *Ceramics in Society*, November 2002:

'Kate Malone, as one would expect, was much more direct and upfront in the way she handled her ceramic room. Completely obliterating the clinical white box with which she was initially presented, she enthusiastically embraced the role of potter as interior decorator, conjuring up a warm, welcoming and comfortable environment, a cosy meeting place for family and friends. Every surface was embellished, from the floor with its crystalline glazed tiles, to the walls and ceiling with their sprigged fruit and leaves, evoking flocked wallpaper plasterwork and prosaic flying ducks. Homely accessories furnished the room, each one a technical *tour de force*, including a sprouting chandelier pulsing with fibre optic lights, and two delicious padded pumpkin pouffes. The centrepiece was a spectacular pineapple fire surround and hearth (complete with firedogs) – significantly, a symbol of hospitality – its generous ogee curves redolent of Islamic art. Whereas Malone's earlier fireplaces were constructed from heavy rectilinear slabs; this one was modelled in low relief, making it livelier and more enticing, drawing you towards it like the mouth-shaped entrance to a fairground ride. Also quietly spectacular were the recessed alcoves, created from two halves of a large vase sliced in half, encrusted with cascading green crystals.

Kate Malone is constantly absorbing and digesting inspirations at a subconscious level. Everything she encounters – in nature, on her global travels, or in everyday life – is potentially grist to the creative mill. A row of pots ranged along a high shelf around the room highlighted the astonishing eclecticism of her sources, which encompass everything from frilly 1960s swimming caps, to fir cones, to ball and spoke atomic models. Although each piece was of a similar size, and some shared the same basic press-moulded body shape, Malone had dressed each pot in a completely different outfit, like a fancy dress parade. First they were swathed in a chunky knitted sweater of applied moulded bulbs or hand-modelled relief decoration; then they were wrapped up in an outdoor coat composed of multiple layers of pebble or crystalline glazes. Closely related to these vessels were several giant pots adorned with garlic bud coats masquerading as items of furniture on the floor. Malone's ability to scale up and down at will, and yet still get the proportions right, is one of her most dazzling skills.'

Bursting Garlic Seed head side table, with Gourd Seat. Double-handled celebration mug and wallpaper sprigs. All stoneware crystalline glazes. Working sketch for seat below.

164

All the fittings and pieces for this room were made from T Material clay, except the crystalline glazed porcelain tiled floor.

Fittings include: floor tiles (20 cm square); skirting-board; door surround; wallpaper sprigs; door window port-hole, door knob and key hole; half-pot top-lit ceramic alcoves set behind holes cut into the wall; ceramic fire surround (made in sections); hearth; fire dogs; pouffe cushions; side table; seat; ceiling light with 'uplight' and fibre optic fittings; ceiling spriggs; small wall shelves; mirror. The high shelf includes 22 (15 cm high) pots each wearing differently modelled coats, a single pineapple vase, and two pairs of small pots.

Materials and equipment

Introduction – Why clay?

My earliest memory of clay is of making a clay fairy cake painted with powder paints when I was six or seven, and loving it. At eleven I went to a big comprehensive school in the suburbs of Bristol. I remember peering through the clay-smeared window of the pottery rooms, wondering what the powders in the jars on the shelves were for. The kiln doors were open, work was dotted all around in a sort of chaotic order, presided over by a handsome, dusty, bohemian teacher, Mr. Eveleigh. After two years' wait – at last a timetable that included pottery! The process of making things in clay was pure pleasure. I was fascinated by the alchemy of change – from soft and wet, to chalky, delicate and dry. Then the transformation to solid ceramic during the biscuit firing, and the way the pale powdery glazes were transformed into rich coloured gloss in the glaze firing. These changes have never ceased to thrill me.

The versatility of clay is wondrous. There are endless different fields to learn about and research. With wood and metal, clay is a material we encounter with such frequency on a daily basis, we tend to take it for granted. It's the earth we walk on, nature itself. In France sun-dried clay is sold in chemists and health shops to take as a medicine and for poultices. Toothpaste, paper, make-up, talcum powder, kaolin and morphine, milk of magnesia – all these everyday things contain clay. We live in houses built of bricks, roofed, floored and clad with ceramic tiles, and serviced by ceramic hobs, basins, loos and drainage pipes.

We eat and drink off ceramic tableware and cook with enamelled pots and pans. Ceramic insulators are key elements of electric pylons and telegraph poles, and our cars run using ceramic spark plugs. Ceramic shields are used in bullet-proof jackets, and on the nose of space rockets and on satellites to reflect the intense heat of the sun. There's a Swiss watch made entirely of clay, except for the glass face, including the strap.

As well as all these, clay is a thing of beauty, used for sculpture, pots and jewellery. For me, it is an absolute honour to be using this versatile material, whose changes are so magical and extreme.

Clay – The basics

Whichever material you use, it is essential to understand its basic characteristics. Once you have acquired this knowledge, you work with the material rather than against it. As a woodworker needs to understand the properties of wood – the strength of the grain; how and why to cut it a certain way, etc. – so a clayworker needs to develop a good understanding of the basic properties of clay. What happens when clay shrinks? Why does clay become shiny when burnished? I originally evolved the explanations that follow as an introduction for student groups and educational workshops, and for individuals on work experience at Balls Pond Studio. This is very basic stuff – my own idiosyncratic explanation of clay as a material, intended purely for novices – so experienced potters may wish to skip this section.

Group of raw unglazed vessels drying beside the kiln. In the centre is a large pumpkin teapot. To the right are two gourds, the tall one at the back with cling film around the rim to prevent it drying too quickly. In the forefront are several kiln firing stilts (crowns).

The tiddlywinks syndrome

Q: What happens when clay shrinks?

Answer: Clay is made up of particles shaped like tiddlywinks. Each tiddlywink has two flat faces and an edge. Each tiddlywink wears two coats in the form of layers of water: a fur coat (free water) and a vest (chemically-combined water). These coats of water have adhesive and cohesive properties which make the tiddlywinks stick together in a tight crowd. This is what makes clay sticky. The more water it contains, the softer the clay, and the greater the shrinkage from wet to bone dry. Each type of clay has different-sized particles, hence the varying rates of shrinkage between different clay bodies.

The first stage of shrinkage takes place when a pot is in its raw state, and the clay starts to dry out in the atmosphere. At this point the tiddly-winks strip off their fur coats (free water) and snuggle up together, ready for the kiln party. Up until this point, the process is reversible.

The second stage of shrinkage takes place during the firing. Now the tiddlywinks strip off their vests (chemically-combined water) and

get really close. This process is irreversible, and brings about the transformation from clay to ceramic.

Understanding the behaviour of clay

Understanding the basic facts about clay shrinkage helps to explain why many other things happen:

Q: Why do tiles or flat slabs warp during drying?

Answer: Particles on one side or around the edge of a tile strip off their fur coats (free water) more quickly than those in the centre. Shrinkage is uneven, and this causes warping, even cracking. The problem can be rectified by various means: wrapping the edges of the tile; turning it over during drying; raising the tile up onto spaced slats of wood as soon as it is stiff enough, so that both surfaces can dry more evenly; sandwiching the tile between surfaces of the same porosity, and sealing the edges; ensuring that drying takes place away from draughts.

Q: What happens when clay is burnished?

Answer: The tiddlywink particles are normally in chaos, bouncing light in all directions from their flat surfaces. When clay is burnished with a spoon or pebble, the tiddlywinks on the surface are laid flat, compressed and put in order, so that their flat surfaces reflect the light and shine.

Q: Why does burnishing disappear when the clay is fired over 900°C-950°C?

Answer: At these temperatures during the biscuit firing the tiddly-

winks have a rave in the kiln. The imposed order is muddled up, the tiddlywinks rearrange themselves again, and the burnishing is lost.

Q: Why are hand-rolled coils stronger than extruded ones?

Answer: The tiddlywinks in an extruded coil are in chaos; the particles are not arranged in any particular order. In hand-rolled coils the tiddlywinks are arranged in order and bound together, and this gives the coil strength. The first stage of binding the tiddlywinks together occurs when a spiral is introduced during wedging. This spiral needs to be continued through into the squeezing of the coil. By compressing the clay against the worktop during the rolling process, the adhesive and cohesive properties of water are maximised. At this stage, if you were to test the strength of the two types of coil by holding them up and swinging them, the hand-rolled coil would be the last to break.

Because of its greater strength and flexibility, the hand-rolled coil is not thinned or weakened by handling when bringing the coil up towards the pot. The advantage of this is that it enables you to use longer coils – especially useful on large-scale pieces – and to have fewer joins between coil ends, which can be weak spots.

Q: Why can seams reappear after a biscuit firing?

Answer: The tiddlywinks can be compressed closely together while the clay is raw, but when they have their party in the kiln, they realign and fight to get their own space. As a result, denser areas of particles can bulge out where pieces of clay have been joined. To make sure this does not happen, seams should be cut away, not compressed, otherwise they may return to haunt you.

Q: When throwing on a wheel, why is the thin wall of clay so strong one minute, yet weakens or collapses the next?
Answer: When clay is centred on the wheel, a sense of order is established between particles, and the tiddlywinks are arranged like soldiers in rows. At this stage the water sticks the tiddlywinks together, making the clay strong. As throwing continues, the pot is pulled outwards and upwards, and surface contact between particles get less and less until – flop! – the weight of the clay is greater than the adhesive strength of the water. The clay is stretched to its limits, the tiddlywinks are exhausted, and the piece collapses.

Some clays are easier to throw with than others, and an experienced thrower learns the limits of each different type of clay. In general terms, this explains why certain clays are better suited than others to being used for particular techniques.

T Material clay

All my work is made from T Material clay, supplied by Thermal Ceramics (UK) Ltd. One of its key ingredients is a high-fired grog that makes the clay tolerant of being used for complex and large-scale forms. I love working with T Material. It suits the slow way in which I make my pots, and gives me the flexibility to carry out multiple glaze firings. Sometimes a half-made piece will sit on my desk wrapped in plastic for several months, but a few sprays with water will bring it back to workable life. Occasionally I have re-fired a pot up to twenty times without the body cracking.

Although T Material is expensive by comparison with other clays – more so even than porcelain – I don't use huge quantities, so the price is not prohibitive. It would probably be more economical to use a different clay on smaller works, but because my studio is fairly small, I prefer to use just one type of clay as this keeps the storage and reclaim process simple. One of the great advantages of T Material is that it keeps its shape even when fired to high temperatures. Also, because it fires fairly white, it provides a light base for coloured glazes, brightening and intensifying their tones.

I use T Material for both earthen-ware and stoneware pieces:

For earthenware, I biscuit fire to 1180°C, then glaze fire to 1040-60°C. The high biscuit firing makes it more difficult to apply glazes, but the advantage is that the pot has a harder finish, rather than the soft spongy texture of low-fired earthenware.

For stoneware, I biscuit fire to 1000°C, then glaze fire up to 1260°C.

Reclaiming clay

When my T Material clay arrives from the suppliers, it is too hard to use. To reclaim it to a workable consistency I make a stack of 4cm thick slices of clay, piled one above the other. Each slice is indented with holes, filled with water. The stack is covered and left overnight, then the next day it is wedged into small lumps, which are stored individually in plastic bags to keep them fresh.

To reclaim small scraps of clay that have not dried out too much, I roll them into a thick even sausage. Then I make deep thumbholes along its length, fill the holes with water, wrap the clay in a bag, leave it overnight, and wedge it back up the following day. The grog in the T Material opens the body up, allowing the water to penetrate it quickly and evenly.

Drying work

Careful drying is crucial because each pot is made slowly and the walls can vary in thickness, often with components of soft clay added to a stiffer core. When a piece is finished, initially it is kept loosely wrapped in plastic for several days, so that the moisture content can equalise throughout the clay. The adhesive and cohesive properties of water assist this migration. The plastic is then loosened gradually, and the piece is kept away from draughts. The first stages of drying are the most important. Taking precautions at this stage paves the way for a more speedy second stage of drying. Once the pot has been uncovered, ideally it should be left for several more days before it is moved. For their final stage of drying, I usually position my pieces in the warmth next to the kiln.

Extremities, such as handles or spouts, are left loosely draped with a piece of plastic, so that they do not dry out before the main body, as this can create stresses within the clay and may cause cracks between constituent parts. As an added precaution I often do a 24 hour 'toasting' in the kiln, prior to the biscuit firing. I heat the kiln very slowly in stages up to about 70°C, hold it there for 4-5 hours, and then let it cool. On the largest pieces 'toasting' can take up to three days. I am probably over-cautious in my drying and firing habits, but I prefer to err on the side of caution because there is so much at stake with labour-intensive pieces.

Equipment, tools and materials

Hacksaw blades

For working the rough clay surfaces into smooth compact curves and edges during and after coiling, I use hacksaw and sabre-saw blades of varying sizes and grades. Bigger sabre-saw blades are handy on larger works, and easier to hold tightly between your fingertips. I buy various grades of tooth from coarse to fine, and use them in that order, gradually removing surface humps and bumps. For fine work I prefer to use older blades, as the teeth soften with use and become finer still. I break them into different lengths so they will fit into awkward spaces. It is quite difficult to exert the necessary cutting pressure on a narrow blade, so you need to develop a strong grip. I use serrated metal kidneys to get into concave areas. Ideally I would like serrated metal fingernails, but these blades are a good substitute.

Rubber kidneys

For smoothing, compressing and burnishing the surface of the clay after it has been evened out with hacksaw blades, I use a selection of rubber kidneys. The kidney-shaped pieces of rubber vary in size, thickness and stiffness. They are really important to create the tight curved surfaces on my pots. I am always on the lookout for the perfect rubber kidney, and I have begged, borrowed and bought many on my travels over the years. Some I have kept since I was at college because they were so perfect. I yearn for a supplier of high quality, crisp-edged kidneys in thick, firm, red rubber, but alas, the rubber used these days is of a much poorer quality than it

used to be, not fine compression-injected but roughly cut. The new kidneys I now find are often too soft or too hard, with rough edges that have to be smoothed off before they can be used. We make them smooth by using them to sieve the glazes, rubbing them against the fine mesh of the sieve until the edges are straight and free of burrs. The thumb is the ideal kidney; mine is worked flat and broad from years of use on rims.

Wooden tools

For modelling, and for compressing grog away from fine edges and modelled details (sometimes through cling film), I use a range of wooden tools. I have four favourites made of boxwood that I have used for twenty years. Sadly, tools do not seem to be made as finely any more. Boxwood is strong and fine-grained, retaining strength and edge, even when wet.

Cling film

I wrap my pots in cling film to keep them keep extra-moist. I also use cling film extensively for modelling or impressing through, and for smoothing the clay on roll top rims. By stretching a layer of cling film over a rim, then compressing the clay surface, there is much less danger of catching the smooth contours with your hand or tools. For modelling, thick strong cling film is best, giving a generous, cushioned, soft impression. If it is too thin, it will burst under pressure. Also, it has to be robust enough to impress through using plaster sprigs or plastic found objects, as on my wheel-thrown Carnival Ware.

Turntables

I have a range of six metal turntables to suit the different sizes of my pots. Most are standard models from ceramic suppliers. The exception is a large custom-designed turntable that I purchased from the potter Monica Young, who specialises in giant coil-built vessels. Made to her specifications and measuring about 35cm high and 45cm in diameter, it is perfectly level and runs incredibly smoothly. Fortunately Monica sold me her spare.

Sundry tools and materials

• Hole makers of various sizes.
• Wire hoops of varying shapes and sizes to hollow out handles and spouts.
• Three or four wooden rolling pins. They get wet and sticky when used, and need to be swapped over.
• Metal comb-like tools, sold in supermarkets as onion slicing devices, ideal for quickly scratching surfaces between coils.
• Spikes and pins on sticks.
• Wire harp for slab preparation and reclaim.
• Loads of newspapers.
• Water sprayer to moisten pots.
• A big roll of plastic dry cleaning covers, bought from a dry-cleaning suppliers, invaluable for preventing pots from drying out when I have got several on the go at one time. Sometimes a piece can sit on the desk half made for six months. As long as it is wrapped in cling film, covered in layers of plastic, and checked and sprayed every few months, it will be fine.

Kiln and kiln furniture

The control box of my beautiful big kiln

Big kiln

I use a large 36 cubic ft. (3ft x 3ft x 4ft) three-phase electric trolley kiln. It has ten programmable ramps of temperature control, and there are three pyrometers, one for each zone of control. This means that, when firing large pots that fill the kiln, an even firing with low differential is guaranteed. The kiln was bespoke-made in Stoke-on-Trent by a firm previously known as Kiln Engineering, now renamed Hot Box. They make kilns of huge dimensions, and mine is one of their smaller models. It is a trolley kiln, where the trolley can come out and be completely wheeled away from the kiln itself. This enables me to take the trolley to the biggest pieces, load them, then wheel it back. Ideally I would like two trolleys, so that large pots could actually be made and dried on them, reducing the traumatic stress and risk of lifting and loading brittle and delicate large pieces into trolley position.

Kiln furniture

Kiln furniture, made from high-fired refractory clay, is used to support the kiln shelves during firing. The shelves support the pots, which are often raised on stilts to prevent them sticking to the shelves. I love the satisfying functional shapes of kiln furniture, but stacking the big kiln with these building blocks and the kiln shelves, then precariously balancing the work on stilts, is a delicate and nerve-racking job. Sometimes there can be three months' work packed in one kiln. This is the part of the process that I like the least. One careless action can destroy months of work. Meticulous checking is necessary and all my powers of concentration are called upon.

Health and safety

Clay and glazes are toxic and dangerous, and should be handled with respect. As I wish to continue using clay for many years to come, I owe it to the environment and to myself to take care. This section does not cover all aspects of health and safety, just a few tips regarding good practice. Anyone wanting further advice should consult appropriate specialist books or suppliers.

Clay

Wet clay is not a problem and we often ingest it as a medicine, but dry clay dust is potentially lethal, as the edge of each disc-shaped particle is razor sharp. The particles of clay dust that you can actually see are just the larger ones. These are generally filtered from the air you breathe by the hairs in your nose. Smaller particles, however, can get past these traps and sneak into your lungs, where they quiver and shred the delicate lung tissues. This is called silicosis, and it can kill you.

Beware of dust and keep it to a minimum. Examine the direction of the airflow in your studio. It is sensible to locate clay reclaim and pot drying areas in the airflow beyond the area where you work. I cringe when I see overalls, aprons, plastic bags or towels caked in dry clay, still being used. Common sense and a very good vacuum cleaner are advised. Sweep as little as possible. It is much better to wet mop or hoover. My vacuum cleaner has two filters to stop the fine dust from being blown back into the atmosphere. To facilitate thorough mopping and vacuum cleaning, I keep as many things as possible off the floor on low trolleys. It is not expensive to make trolleys using shuttering plywood or MDF, with small wheels at each corner. Wherever you create dust or use dry powders, spray the air immediately with a fine water spray to catch the particles and send them down to the ground.

Glazes

Whenever I handle glazes or make plaster moulds, I always use a good quality dust mask and wear surgical gloves. I also use a barrier cream, making sure to rub it into the cuticles and behind the nails, as it is through these parts of the body in particular that toxic materials can easily enter the blood stream. I always put dry powders into water as soon as possible when weighing out glazes. When I do a serious batch of glazing I take full of spectrum of vitamin tablets, as these help to eject toxins out of the body. Always wash aprons and towels after glazing. It is dangerous stuff.

Glazes

Coloured earthenware glazes

When I was at the Royal College of Art during the mid 1980s I carried out a series of original glaze tests with fellow student Esperanza Romero. These glaze tests formed the basis of the coloured earthenware glazes that I have continued to use ever since. The tests were simple. We took a ready-made clear earthenware glaze and experimented by adding various colouring agents. Because the base glaze was high in borax, it rendered colours beautifully bright. The glaze we chose has a wide firing range between 1000°C and 1120°C. The higher it is fired, the more fluid it becomes in the kiln. As a standard we fired the tests to 1060°C. I often use ready-made products as a starting point for research; as a constituent ingredient this can save a lot of time. Using a ready-made glaze is more expensive than mixing your own, but as I do not produce work in huge quantities, the price of materials is not so much of an issue.

The ready-made glaze was food safe as supplied, but with additions this can change. When I started using this glaze on my short-run studio production Carnival Ware, I sent a sample to a glaze-testing laboratory to have the addition of cobalt (for blue) and iron (for honey) tested for food safety, as these are the colours I use on the inside of functional domestic wares. As this range was intended for food or drink, I wanted to be sure that it would not harm the user. It is the responsibility of functional ceramics producers to check the food safety of the glazes they use. Copper green glazes are often poisonous at earthenware temperatures, and should not be applied on the inside of pots that might be used for salad dressing or acidic fruit juices. Copper activates the release of lead in earthenware glazes, which is highly dangerous to health.

Coloured earthenware glaze test programme

For our programme of glaze tests, Esperanza and I worked out a plan together, making duplicate tests and halving the workload. We started with simple additions of single colouring agents in varying amounts. Using a base of 100g of clear glaze, we tried adding the following in various percentages:

Cobalt oxide	
0.2%, 0.4%, 0.6%, 0.8%, 1%, 5%	
Cobalt carbonate	as above
Copper carbonate	
2%, 4%, 6%, 8%, 10%	
Copper oxide	as above
Vanadium pentoxide	as above
Rutile light	as above
Manganese dioxide	as above
Black nickel oxide	as above
Red iron oxide	as above
Black iron oxide	as above
Tin oxide	as above

Once we had completed all the single blend tests, we started to combine two different colourants with the clear glaze. For example, copper carbonate with iron, copper with cobalt, copper with vanadium, copper with rutile, and so on, until all the various different combinations of pairs had been tried. Each pair of colourants was tried out in four to six different tests within that combination.

After leaving college I continued carrying out glaze tests on my own, making blends of three colourants, such as copper and iron and copper; copper and cobalt and vanadium. The possibilities were endless. To introduce colour, I also tested glaze stains in various proportions on their own, and tried blending these with oxides and carbonates. The result was to customise and soften the range of ready-made colours commonly used by other potters. For example, adding a touch of red iron oxide softens a bright yellow glaze stain; and adding copper carbonate to a yellow glaze stain makes an emerald green, sometimes containing soft yellow bubbles. These tests were used on the pots I was making at the time, the glazaes on my work reflected the palette I was testing.

I also made experiments to change the surface texture of the glaze by adding china clay, slips and various ready-made products, such as 'Snowfall' glazes (see pages 34, 36 and 111). All the glaze tests were fired at an angle to illustrate the flux changes made by the additions. This is very important, as it has evolved that I exploit the movement of the glaze during firing as a feature of my work. As a result of this extensive programme of glaze testing, I am now able to call upon around 1500 earthenware colours and textures, all developed around this one ready-made glaze. This flexibility is particularly useful when I work on projects with architects or interior designers where colour scheme is part of the brief.

Carnival ware glazes

The basic set of recipes that I use on my Carnival Ware is as follows:

Rich copper green:
6% copper carbonate added to 100g clear glaze

Deep blue:
2% cobalt carbonate added to 100g clear glaze

Turquoise:
6% copper carbonate added to 50g high alkaline frit and 50g clear glaze

Honey:
6% red iron oxide added to 100g clear glaze

Blue green:
0.5% cobalt carbonate and 2% copper carbonate added to 100g clear glaze

Pearly white:
6% vanadium pentoxide

Olive green:
4% copper carbonate and 4% red iron oxide added to 100g clear glaze

For apple greens, pinks, yellows, lilacs and oranges:
general 6% to 8% glaze stain added to 100g clear glaze

I enjoy observing and exploiting the inherent characteristics of a glaze. For example, added ingredients can affect the degree of glaze fluidity in the kiln, causing either fluxing or stiffening. They can also affect the transparency or opacity of a glaze. In my Carnival Ware range I exploit subtle differences such as these to enhance the shapes of the vessels and the impressed decoration. For example, the honey, turquoise and green glazes that I use on this range are all tinted, but remain transparent, as the colourants have dissolved within the glaze. I apply these colours on the fine impressed relief details, where they highlight particular features, making them shine out. By contrast, on the flatter areas I apply glazes that are more opaque, in other words the yellows, oranges, pinks and lilacs coloured with glaze stain additions. In these glazes the colourants are held in suspension within the glassy matrix, causing a cloudy effect. If opaque colours were used on the impressed areas, they would look clumsy and hide the fine details.

Glaze application

I apply glazes by hand using a variety of brushes, ranging from soft mops to flat finches. This technique originally evolved from lack of funds and equipment after I left college. Now it is my preferred method, being much less noisy and more relaxing by comparison to spraying, as well as much safer with regard to health. Using brushes has also enabled me to develop the technique of overlaying glazes, as well as other subtleties, such as varying the thickness of the glaze on the same piece.

My earthenware pieces are biscuit-fired to quite a high temperature (1180°C), so they are not very porous. I therefore mix my glazes thickly, pushing them through a 120 mesh sieve with a rubber kidney. Layers of glaze are built up gradually using gentle brush strokes. A thick first layer is painted on using a soft flat brush. When this layer is dry, a second layer is painted on, rather more quickly and gently than the first, so as not to disturb the base layer. The piece is then glaze-fired, and the process is repeated until a thick even coat is achieved.

To re-glaze on a piece that has already had a glaze firing, I use calcium chloride as a glaze thickener to stop the glaze from running down the pot. Calcium chloride is sold in flake form, which is mixed into a solution with hot water. A few drops added to a plastic cup of glaze transform it from single cream to whipped cream consistency, making it much easier to paint onto a vertical non-porous surface. Care must be taken, however, as too much calcium chloride produces the opposite effect. I only thicken the amount I am going to use during that glaze session, as the thickening is simply a flocculation that is not real. Flocculation means that the suspension of particles does not actually increase; each particle is simply dressed in a thick, rubbery jacket that sticks to its neighbour, creating only the illusion of thickness. Consequently, an extra thick coat of glaze has to be applied if using calcium chloride.

Earthenware Pebble glazes

Pebble glaze is an American-produced special effect glaze, available ready-mixed from ceramic suppliers (such as Ceramatech in London), who describe it as a 'white glaze that creates a pebbled surface effect'. Basically it contains some kind of elastic properties, which cause it to fragment and curl up into individual bobbles (pebbles) during firing. I fell in love with this glaze effect as soon as I saw it, as it has strong natural associations, like the pattern on the inside of an orchid or foxglove, the skin of a squid or the surface of a shell. I have tried to work out what makes pebble glaze curl up, as it is expensive to use in any quantity, but so far with little success.

Pebble glaze tests

I purchase Pebble glaze in wet form in small 4oz pots. It is only supplied in white. As with the ready-made clear earthenware glaze used as the basis for my coloured glazes, this pre-prepared pebble glaze has been employed as the starting point for a series of coloured glaze tests. I have made a series of tests using Pebble over thick layers of coloured

earthenware glazes, and also over coloured slips. To create different coloured Pebble glazes I add glaze stains or oxides in varying quantities to the basic white pebble glaze. Generally 4 to 8g of glaze stain added to a 4oz pot of Pebble glaze gives a good strong colour. Colour pigment is wetted very slightly and gradually incorporated into the Pebble glaze by gentle thorough stirring. Often I apply Pebble glaze as a top layer over a triple-fired richly coloured earthenware glaze base. (See page 188.)

Creating varied colours and textures using Pebble glazes

Pebble glaze is applied with a fairly stiff flat brush in smooth gentle short strokes. Endless colour and texture combinations can be created with pebble glazes, which are really exciting to play with. I particularly enjoy juxtaposing contrasting effects on different surfaces of the same piece. (See pages 88-9.) Strangely, though, a good colour combination on a small piece sometimes looks completely different on a large pot, so it is important to take account of scale. Here is an outline of some of the other effects I have discovered:

The more thickly the Pebble glaze is applied, the larger each island of pebble on the finished piece.

By varying the thickness of the Pebble glaze, subtle changes can be created in the scale of the islands, producing effects such as the illusion of a flat surface swelling up towards you, like a sliced fruit bursting with juice.

Firing the Pebble glaze with a 4-5 minute soak will make the glaze ooze over the contours of the piece

like a stream of lava. (See pages 50-51.)

Over-firing the glaze can cause the clearly defined pebble pattern to breakdown and melt, creating marbled treacly effects. (See pages 52-3.)

Applying Pebble glaze over a layer of dry slip has completely the opposite effect, causing the formation of lots of individual glassy bobbles over a matt ground, like raindrops on a windowpane. (See page 85.) Be warned, though, this can be tricky to apply.

Pebble glaze can also sit underneath other transparent tinted glazes.

Sometimes I fire a second pebble layer over an already fired pebble coating, which produces softer and more complex colour effects.

Applying several layers of Pebble glaze in the same firing creates one colour island with a different coloured edge, like an aerial view of a Caribbean Island with a beach fanning out into the sea.

Different pigment additions can flux the Pebble glaze to varying degrees, and can be used to advantage.

Crystalline stoneware glazes

Naturally occurring mineral crystals, such as diamonds, emeralds and coal, form in the earth's crust when particular combinations of materials are subjected to specific environmental conditions, including changes of temperature. Crystalline glazes and firings artificially simulate some of these natural conditions. Carefully concocted glaze recipes are treated to rigorously controlled firing cycles, which activate crystals to seed and grow on the surface of the pot within the glassy matrix. In the same way that sugar crystals form when over-saturated solutions of sugar and water are over boiled in the making of toffee or jam, glaze crystals form when an over-saturated glaze solution 'over boils' in the kiln during the controlled cooling cycle of a glaze firing.

The crystals in crystalline glazes vary enormously in size, shape and colour, depending on the specific ingredients in the glaze and the particular features of the firing cycle. For me, crystalline glazes add yet another layer of magic to the alchemy of the ceramic process. Even now each time I open the kiln door after a crystalline glaze firing, I can't believe the transformations that have taken place. Crystalline glazes can be extremely dramatic, and for some potters they become an overwhelming feature of their pots. My aim, though, is to create a balance between form and surface, a harmony between the shape of the body and the glaze surface. When a pot is covered with a thick blanket of glittering crystals, the associations can be rather kitsch, like 1970s disco wallpaper. But crystals also evoke natural associations, resembling butterfly wings, weathered lichen or frost on a windowpane. I enjoy exploiting and crossing these associations. The way I use crystalline glazes reflects the mélange of my own tastes.

I was first stimulated to experiment with crystalline glazes when working on a commission for the architect Nigel Coates. He invited me to produce a large group of ceramic accessories for a fish tank in a hotel in Japan. Worried that my low temperature glazes might leech poison into the warm salt water and kill the fish, I began to research higher temperature glazes. On consulting Emmanuel Cooper's book of glaze recipes I found a basic crystalline glaze recipe. I carried out one test and was hooked. The difference in surface quality and clarity between low-fired earthenware glazes and high-fired stoneware glazes was immediately apparent. Each have their own beauty, but the higher temperature glazes are infinitely superior in terms of sharpness and crispness. Using crystalline glazes and firing my pots to stoneware temperatures meant that I had to improve my making skills, as these higher temperature firings are totally unforgiving of any blemishes on or weaknesses in the making of a piece. The transparency and increased shrinkages of crystalline glazes exaggerate cracks and defects, whereas with earthenware glazes these can quite easily be covered up.

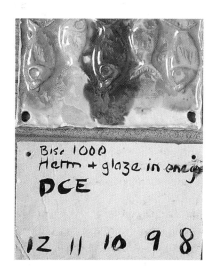

Crystalline glaze testing technique

I used Emmanuel Cooper's alkaline frit base glaze as a starting point for developing a series of coloured crystalline glaze tests, using a similar methodology to that adopted in my glaze tests at the RCA. (See page 174.) I also read a detailed article on crystalline glazes published in *Ceramic Review* by Derek Clarkson, who has spent many years conducting experiments in this field. This provided me with further base recipes around which to test. I also visited Derek Clarkson at his studio. He was extremely generous with information and advice. His attitude towards sharing

Glazes

technical knowledge is exemplary. I try to emulate this by making my research available to anyone who might be interested. The more potters share the results of their experiments, the more our field will develop.

I plan my test tiles so they will yield as much information as possible, such as how the glaze behaves on both horizontal and vertical surfaces; how it varies when thickly or thinly applied; what it looks like applied over another glaze or slip; and the effects of firing to different temperatures within its melt range.

Crystalline Glaze Recipes

Emmanuel Cooper Alkaline Frit base glaze:

Alkaline frit 2962	58g
Zinc oxide	23g
Flint	17g
Bentonite	2g

I like this glaze as the crystals are quiet and reserved, only seen on close inspection.

My additions to Emmanuel Cooper Alkaline Frit base glaze:

Black nickel oxide 1.5g
Honey glaze with electric blue crystals.

Copper carbonate 2g
Light soft turquoise glaze with white/turquoise crystals.

Copper carbonate 6g
Strong emerald green glaze with green crystals.

Copper carbonate 3g
Cobalt carbonate 2g
Greeny blue glaze and crystals.

Cobalt carbonate 2g
Vanadium pentoxide 8g
Transparent glaze with electric blue crystals when thick. Changing the amount of cobalt to 0.4g produces a soft blue glaze with occasional pearly blue patches.

Cobalt carbonate 0.4g
Red iron oxide 3g
Strong deep navy blue glaze with electric blue crystals.

Red iron oxide 3g
Copper carbonate 2g
Olive honey green glaze with slightly darker crystals.

Copper carbonate 2g
Red iron oxide 6g
Honey glaze with honey crystals.

Manganese dioxide 2g-6g
Soft to dark rich brown glaze with paler brown crystals.

Derek Clarkson Base Glaze

Ferro frit 3110	43.9g
Zinc oxide	26.5g
Flint (dry weight)	20.4g
Titanium dioxide	7.8g
China clay	1.42g

When this glaze is used thickly, you get a blanket of crystals, if you are lucky. When it is thin, it produces a mottled glaze with a streaky cream ground.

My additions to Derek Clarkson base glaze:

Cobalt carbonate 0.4g
Manganese dioxide 1.2g
Grey-blue blanket of crystals when thick; pink cream streaky glaze when thin.

Cobalt carbonate 0.4g
Red iron oxide 2g
Pale electric blue crystals when thick, aubergine brown and milky pink glaze when thin.

Copper carbonate 2g
Soft green blanket of crystals when thick; same as above when thin.

Manganese dioxide 2g
Golden brown crystals when thick; tan and cream streaks when thin.

Cobalt carbonate 0.4g
Manganese dioxide 2g
Rich aubergine and cream streaked glaze with soft blue crystals, if you are lucky.

Cobalt carbonate 2g
Manganese dioxide 1.6g
As above, with stronger blue crystals.

Golden yellow high firing glaze stain 2g. Yellow crystals when thick; milky white mottled pink when thin.

Rutile light 2g
Red iron oxide 6g
Dark metallic green crystals when thick; rich dark tan brown with milky olive green runs when thin.

Vanadium pentoxide 6g
Cobalt carbonate 2g
Blue crystals in green-grey glaze when thick; grey and warm cream in rivulets when thin.

For further technical information on crystalline glazes, please refer to the following books, articles and websites:

Derek Clarkson, 'The Crystal Maze', *Ceramic Review*, 137, 1992

Emmanuel Cooper, *Cooper's Book of Glaze Recipes*, Batsford, London, 1987

Emmanuel Cooper, *Glazes*, Batsford, London, 1992

Diane Creber, *Crystalline Glazes*, A & C Black, London, 1997

Mimi Dann, 'Crystalline Glazes', *Ceramic Review*, 128, 1991

Peter Ilsley, *Macro-Crystalline Glazes – The Challenge of Crystals*, Crowood Press, Marlborough, 1999

Bevan Norkin, 'Crystalline Glazes: A Precise Method', *Ceramics Monthly*, March 1992

Fara Shimbo, *Crystal Glazes – Understanding the Process and Materials*, eBook published by Digitalfire Corporation, Alberta, Canada (see www.crystalglazes.info and www.digitalfire.com

Applying and firing crystalline glazes

Application: The glazes are mixed very thickly, and passed through a 120 mesh sieve, which takes a long time. I store them in lidded buckets. I apply the glazes thickly towards the top of the piece and more thinly at the base. What seems to work best is applying one coat all over, a second coat on the top two thirds, and a third coat on the top third. Finally I ooze some more glaze on the uppermost points, bearing in mind the projected movement of the glaze over the contours of the pot during the firing. The glaze is applied so thickly that it cracks and curls, and often falls off in lumps, which need to be repainted or glued back on with more glaze. The pot looks rather a mess as it goes into the kiln, but the intended results are firmly fixed in my mind.

Trays and stilts: Crystalline glazes run like mad in the kiln, and crystal growth is partly stimulated by the movement of the glaze down and over the pot. Each pot has to have its own glaze tray to catch the highly corrosive drips. If the piece is very heavy or difficult to balance, I make a bespoke stilt to hold it above the tray and kiln shelf.

Firing cycle: A normal glaze firing involves carefully controlling the temperature rise to the correct level, then turning the kiln off and letting it cool naturally. With crystalline glaze firings, the cooling of the kiln is also controlled between approximately 1100°C to 1000°C. My own magic numbers are 1093°C to 1069°C. It is during this period that the over-saturation of the solution occurs and crystals grow. The overall length and pattern of the cooling cycle will affect the size and shape of the crystals.

My typical crystalline glaze firing cycle is as follows:

60°C per hour to 180°C
70°C per hour to 300°C
100°C per hour to 600°C
Raise to 1260°C as fast as possible
Drop to 1100°C as fast as possible
Hold at 1100°C for 40 mins
Drop to 1093°C as fast as possible
Hold at 1093°C for 20 mins
Drop to 1083°C as fast as possible
Hold at 1083°C for 30 mins
Drop to 1069°C as fast as possible
Hold at 1069°C for 15 mins
Raise to 1093°C as fast as possible
Hold at 1093°C for 15 mins
Turn off kiln and allow to cool as normal.

The slow cooling around these temperatures stimulates the crystals to grow; the rise in temperature at the end can create halos around each crystal. If you were to raise and drop the temperature several times within the controlled cooling period, you would create more and more halos around the original seeded crystals. However, crystalline glazes are complex and unpredictable, and there are many other variables to consider:

The position of the pot in the kiln. It is usually hottest at the top of the kiln.

The speed at which the temperature in your kiln is capable of rising.

New elements will heat the kiln more quickly, causing less glaze to slip down the piece. This generally produces better results.

The problem with old elements is that the kiln heats up more slowly, causing more glaze to run down off the pot. This results in a thinner layer of glaze, with seeds for crystals pulled to the base of the pot. They may even fall right off the piece, and you will end up with a drip tray full of lovely crystals.

The more densely the kiln is packed, the slower it will cool. Generally this causes better crystal growth.

Crystals tend to grow better on the inside of pots, where the cooling is slower.

Crystals will grow dramatically in pools on a flat surface.

Packing the kiln and grinding bases

The extreme runniness of crystalline glazes during firings causes obvious problems. Most pots end up with a stilt or prop of some kind stuck to their base after firing. They may even weld themselves to a kiln shelf if they tilt or warp during the firing. The more care taken when making the stilts and the more care taken when propping the pots in the kiln, the less grinding work will be needed afterwards. Pieces should be balanced on as small a surface area of the prop as possible, although shrinkage and movement of the pots, and sometimes a redistribution of weight due to glaze movement, can cause unforeseen problems. For me, packing the big kiln for a crystalline glaze firing is the most nerve-racking stage of the whole process of making ceramics. Sometimes there may be several months of work in a single firing, with shelves and pots packed high, and work wobbling precariously on kiln furniture and the tiny points of stilts. I always hold my breath when opening the kiln door after a firing, praying not to see the work in a pile at the bottom of the kiln, or tilted and stuck together in a pack.

The base of each piece invariably has to have its surface smoothed off with an angle grinder, then polished with diamond pads or small grinding stones. I mark the blemishes with a gold pen or gold leaf to indicate that I knew that they were there.

Angle grinders are dangerous tools, and I am fortunate that my partner Graham does this job for me. It is nerve-racking to turn a delicate piece of work upside down and work into it with such a large violent instrument, especially with large pots. I wrap intricate pieces of work in cling film before grinding to prevent the fine dust from lodging in the details.

Happy accidents

Happy accidents are the unplanned things that happen to your work, the unexpected surprises. Mine have been mostly been to do with glazes. The first time this happened was during my BA at Bristol Polytechnic during the early 1980s. I had decided to set myself the task of slip-casting a dozen mugs, and I wanted them to be as perfect in quality as factory-made mugs. They were decorated with a sprayed underglaze tiger coat pattern, intended to be sharp and graphic. In my ignorance or haste, however, I had not fixed the stencil-sprayed underglaze with gum or a pre-firing, and I immediately over-sprayed it rather thickly with clear glaze. In the kiln the thick glaze grabbed the black tiger camouflage pattern, and they both slipped downwards. When I opened the kiln and saw the dragged pattern, initially I was disappointed. However, I soon realised that the effect was like a tiger's fur, and the dragging was a bonus rather than a failure. This important early happy accident strongly influenced the way I now work with glazes.

What I discovered is that you need to use the natural elements of the ceramic process to your advantage, to work with them rather than against them. On many of my pieces the movement of the glaze over the contours of a piece accentuates the underlying form. As a result, form and surface are married in a symbiotic relationship.

Often I take glaze movement to extremes, letting coloured rivers of glaze ooze over the form. The glaze does the work for me when melting at the top temperature of the firing, although there is a fine line between creating an inspired piece and producing a blurry mess.

When firing glazes there are many nuances to consider: the glaze application technique; the thickness and fluidity of the glaze; the angle of the pot's surface; the position of the piece in the kiln; the speed of the firing cycle. All these factors need to be considered, and can be used to advantage in the finished piece. However, it is equally crucial to recognise the importance of happy accidents. Keep an open mind, otherwise their significance could quite easily pass you by.

Press-moulding a Double-Walled Sliced Fruit of Your Dreams

Using press moulds to repeat shapes enables me to reduce production costs and create mid-price pieces. This section illustrates the process of making a double-walled Sliced Fruit of Your Dreams. The original piece from which the two-part plaster mould was taken was hand-built in a similar way to the Pea Pod illustrated on page 184.

Although the piece illustrated here is fairly small and simple, this mould-filling technique of filling a press mould works well for larger and more complex moulds, making light work of a potentially heavy task. I originally developed the 'patchwork' technique in order to avoid handling large sheets of clay.

I prepare the slabs of clay needed to line the mould by cutting them with a wire harp from a larger block of clay that has been thoroughly wedged.

Choosing the correct stiffness of clay is paramount. Being sensitive to the subtle properties of clay and making the correct judgements can save a lot of time.

I like the clay to be quite soft so that I do not need to use any water on the joints whilst filling the mould, as water creates areas of uneven consistency.

To increase handling strength of a wire-cut slab, I gently roll and compress the surface with a rolling pin.

I line the mould with a patchwork of pieces, making sure that the joins between each

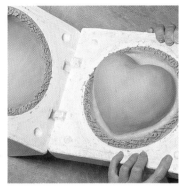

piece are deeply scratched on both edges. The patchwork must be properly knitted together by overlapping each piece slightly, and then by pushing hard backwards and forwards across the joints with my fingers.

Once the mould has been patchwork lined and worked with metal and rubber kidneys, the inside surface is smoothed through a layer of cling film.

At this stage it is easy to make the mistake of pushing the clay around the mould, making the walls uneven in thickness. To guard against this, I test the depth of the walls at regular intervals using a spike to gauge whether there is an even layer throughout the clay.

It is important to develop a feel for subtle differences, such as gauging the depth of clay in a mould, the thickness of a pot, or the correct weight of clay for a certain job. Fine-tuning is the key to a successful pot. These qualities feed through directly into the touch and feel of the finished piece.

With this piece I cannot get into the interior after closing the mould, so I have to be sure that the angles of the clay edges are exactly right before putting the

two halves together. Determining these angles is common sense; there should be enough clay on both halves for a good meeting of surfaces, creating a strong bond. Too much clay on the edges will prevent the mould from closing.

The joining edges are deeply scratched and wetted slightly before putting the sections together.

Once out of the mould, the outside seams from the patchwork of slabs are scratched with a fine blade, slightly wetted, then filled using a narrow coil pressed firmly into the cuts. This is crucial to achieve 'invisible seams'. The piece is then wrapped in plastic and left for the moisture to equalise.

With press-moulding it is tempting to assume that most of the work is over once the piece has been removed from the mould. However, with my pieces there are still several hours of hand work to do.

Finishing the surface involves a series of sweeps using hacksaw blades and rubber kidneys. This process is repeated three times, each sweep refining the surface of the piece even more. Finally a rubber kidney is

used to smooth the almost burnished surface.

I use a spirit level throughout the cleaning up process to ensure the piece is level. During the glaze firing, to prevent the glazes running, it has to be stilted level.

The small size and apparent simplicity of this piece belie the fact that it is one of the most difficult of the press-moulded editions to make.

Step by Step 2

Building a roll top rim

Roll top rims are a recurrent feature of my work. To make them I need to roll an absolutely perfect coil of clay. Here are my tips for how to do this. Carefully chose the correct consistency of clay for the job, then wedge it. Too stiff and the coil will dry out too quickly whilst rolling and the surface will crack on application. Too soft and the clay will be too sticky and the coil will over respond to your touch.

In the photo the darker moist patches indicate how much of my hands I use to start a coil.

Practise rolling a coil over and over again until you get it right.

Sometimes it is easier to roll the clay with your eyes closed, feeling where you need to exert pressure to refine the coil as it takes shape.

Towards the end of the process I slow down and pay attention to problem areas, rolling with one or two fingers to exert pressure where needed.

I roll the coil slowly and lengthen it in stages, working from the middle outwards so as to avoid hollow ends. Small hollows inevitably form, which I pinch away at regular intervals.

The smoothest surface will be created where the coil has been rolled against the desk, rather than where it has contact with your fingers, which invariably leave marks. Towards the end I turn the coil over so that the blemishes face the worktop, trying to avoid marking the clay again with my fingers. This is a tricky business, and one side of the coil is always better than the other.

After the firm top edge of the pot is worked level and even, the coil is sliced along its length, and the flat surface of the half coil is scratched quite deeply in two directions.

The top outer edge of the pot is also scratched, then lightly wetted with a paintbrush, and scratched again to produce localised slurry.

The half coil is placed against the pot's top outer edge, and pressed firmly on whilst rotating the pot on a turntable.

  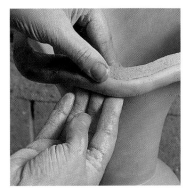 

If the top has a wavy rim, care must be taken not to stretch the coil into the concave areas, as this may cause cracks during firing.

The same applies where the coil joins up full circle; the ends must not be stretched towards each other, or they will pull back, revealing a join as it dries.

The whole rim area is then tightly covered with cling film, and the half coil is firmly bonded onto the piece. Working through the cling film with the palm of the hand facilitates a firm, sweeping, smoothing action. The pot, with the cling film still in place, is then wrapped in plastic and left for a few days. This allows the moisture to equalise slowly between the soft coil and the firm pot.

The sharp top inner edge is then slowly worked away using hacksaw blades. Smoothing with fingers and rubber kidneys completes the luscious rolling rim.

Roll top rims are intended to suggest a spirit of generosity, where the pot's inner surface rolls outwards, freely offering up its inner space – like a human lip.

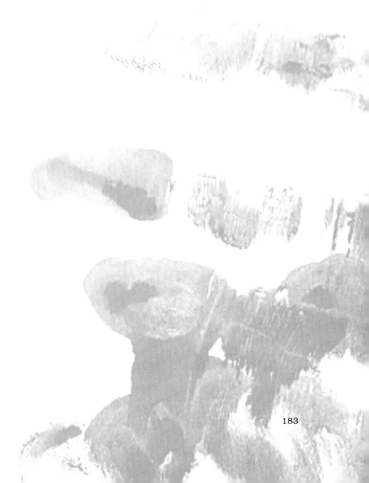

Step by Step 3

Hand-building a Double-Walled Pea Pod

I make four pinch pot bowl shapes and leave them to stiffen.

When they are firm enough to handle I make sure that the insides are perfectly smooth, and work the rims flat with a hacksaw blade.

Next, I draw round the bowls to record their exact shape, and make a paper pattern of the pod I want to make.

I trace this onto a wooden board and lay the bowls face down into the correct position. At this stage I am working on the piece upside down.

Working against the board, I build coils around and in between the bowls to create the flat top area of the pod, following the outline marked on the board.

To start building the outside wall I lay concentric coils along the edge of the flat top section.

I use thick, soft hand-rolled coils, and once they are in position I squeeze and pinch them to make them thinner and work them into the correct shape.

Normally I work two coils, then let them stiffen overnight, resuming the next day.

I keep building up rows of coils until the outer wall is nearly closed.

Before I plug the opening I let the main body dry to quite hard, so the last piece of clay can be pushed against it quite firmly to ensure that it is properly bonded. With a double-walled piece the shrinkage strains are greater. The plug is a weak point where cracks may appear.

Once the outer wall is finished I wrap the piece in plastic for a few days to let the moisture equalise throughout.

Then I clean up the still exposed bottom side with a series of sweeps with hacksaw blades, using rubber kidneys to make the surface perfectly smooth.

The piece is left unwrapped to stiffen so that it can be turned over onto a piece of foam.

Then I scratch the seams between the newly revealed coils on the upturned surface, and fill them with thin coils of clay. Again the piece is wrapped and left overnight.

Next, I work the top, side and inner bowls with hacksaw blades and rubber kidneys to smooth the surfaces.

The stem is modelled separately and hollowed out, then joined to the pod and smoothed.

A 'beaded' edge is added to the rim of the pod by joining a thin coil sliced along its length.

I work through cling film, which helps the fingers and tools slide, press over contours and clarify edges and lines.

I make one small hole in the piece to let air out of the inside chamber. In the kiln a sealed air space is likely to explode during firing.

The piece is wrapped for a few days, then left to dry slowly, away from draughts.

Because it has a double wall, drying needs to be slower than usual. To ensure it is completely

dry before biscuit firing, it sits for a day in the kiln set at a very low temperature (70°C).

As this piece is going to be high-fired to stoneware and decorated with crystalline glazes, a clay tray and props are made to fit the shape of the pod, fired to the same biscuit temperature. The tray consists of a slab with upturned edges, resembling an empty pastry case. The tray will catch the glaze drips that inevitably fall from the pot during the glaze firing.

This type of piece has to be carefully stilted so that it is perfectly level in the kiln to prevent glaze running down the sides and ensure a rich crystal pool of glaze on the top.

I paint the glazes on with big soft brushes.

I start on the base, keeping in mind that this needs coverage but no great thickness, as most of this glaze will run off the pot during the firing.

The piece is turned the correct way up and glaze is applied to the stem.

Crystals grow best on horizontal surfaces where they can pool.

Overlaying the different glazes creates exciting new mixes of crystals and colours.

I apply the glazes in very thick patches on the flat top surface, so thick that the dry glaze coating cracks like mud in a riverbed.

The piece is set onto its tray with stilts and fired to 1260°C.

Step by Step 4

 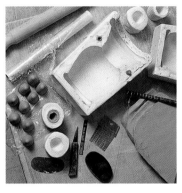 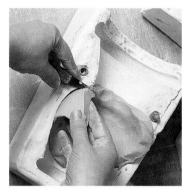 

Making a Small Tutti Frutti Vase

The spikes on the Tutti Frutti range are individually press-moulded in a one-part drop out mould, cast from the tip of a pointed light bulb. Experiments with other bulb shapes have resulted in the Blackberry and Brussels Sprout pots and the Atomic pieces.

I prepare the slabs for filling the moulds.

The two-part plaster mould for this vase was taken from a coil-built original.

The slabs are bent roughly into shape and laid into the vase mould, patchwork fashion.

See page 181 for details of this process.

The two halves of the mould are carefully filled and the edges are prepared.

The depth of the walls is checked using a needle tool to ensure they an even thickness.

Filling the mould takes at least an hour on this small piece.

The mould is squeezed hard closed and left for a short while.

Then one half of the mould is removed, and the pot is lifted out.

Seams and cracks on the inner and outer surfaces are scratched, then filled with thin coils of clay.

The piece is wrapped in plastic, then left for at least a day to let the moisture equalise throughout the clay.

The vase is then cleaned up using hacksaw blades and rubber kidneys.

Tools with long handles are used to clean up the inside, as the neck is too narrow to get my hand inside.

Rows and rows of hollow press-moulded spikes are prepared. To speed up production, four identical light bulb moulds are normally used.

This is the smallest vessel in the Tutti Frutti range, and it requires about sixty spikes. The bigger pieces need hundreds of spikes. To make life easier we use precision electric scales to weigh out the right amount of clay needed for each ball to be pressed into each bulb spike.

We are aiming for a perfect tight pressing without any blemishes. If the clay is too dry when it is pushed into the narrow deep mould, it will develop a wrinkled 'elephant skin' surface. If it is too wet, the clay will quickly saturate the small mould, causing each pressing to stick in the mould.

Each spike needs to be made to 'cuddle up' to its neighbours, so that there is a sense of them growing together as one.

When a bulb is pulled from the mould it has a round open base. Before it can be joined to the body, each base needs to be trimmed and shaped to fit exactly against the other bulbs already joined.

The joining on of the spikes continues in rings down the piece. I try not to make the pattern too regular as changes in rhythm are important.

The spikes diminish in size towards the base as a result of trimming them shorter. This gives a sense of organic growth and, on a practical level, make the rows nestle tightly towards the foot.

Each spike is hollow and needs a breather hole where it joins the body, created using a needle tool bent at an angle. I usually make two or three tiny holes in each hollow spike in case the thick glazes block them up.

Once the making stage is complete, the piece is plastic wrapped to let the moisture equalise through the clay for several days. Then the pot is dried slowly, and biscuit-fired to 1180°C.

For technical details of the glazes on this piece, see pages 174-6.

Glaze is poured inside the vessel and swilled around to ensure full coverage.

The inside of this piece is yellow – intended to suggest that the sun is shining from the interior space.

Different glaze colours are applied to different areas using a brush.

Because I am trying to produce an exceptionally thick layer of colour, three separate glaze firings are required. The same colour glaze is re-applied where needed each time, fired to 1060°C.

The thick layer cannot be achieved in a single glaze firing, as ugly pinholes appear. I try to avoid the glaze becoming gloopy, hence the gradual selected build up over three firings.

Because the glaze moves when it melts during the firing, measures have to be taken to compensate for this. For example, I vary the thickness of the glaze so that it does not collect under the rim or spikes.

The pot is re-glazed and the colour thickened where needed.

Once the desired thickness of plain glaze colour has been achieved, special effect pebble glazes are applied.

Five different Pebble colours are used on this pot. No two adjacent spikes are the same colour.

To achieve the desired textural effects, three separate coats of pebble glaze have to be applied. Painting on these finishing layers takes at least a full day.

Lilac pebble glaze is applied over a triple-fired base of plain lilac glaze.

For an illustration of a completed piece, see page 82 (centre).

Balls Pond Studio

During my seven years at college I was surrounded by extensive equipment, and I developed a taste for making large-scale ceramics. Afterwards I was determined to continue in this vein, and my ambition to make large pots meant acquiring a big kiln of my own. My partner Graham Inglefield and I had the idea of creating a communal studio, equipped so that I could undertake major ceramic projects, as well as providing facilities for others. In 1989, using land at the back our house in Hackney, we built and developed Balls Pond Studio. The small building eventually provided shared workshop space for up to fourteen ceramists, and housed one of the largest studio kilns in London. Rather than being a profit-making commercial enterprise, the

primary aim of Balls Pond Studio was to provide affordable studio space, and many of the workspaces were rented out on a time-share basis in order to keep rents down. The age of members ranged from 18 to 70, and there were often five or six different nationalities working under the one roof. Balls Pond Studio was recognised as a flagship model for other shared studios. During its operation it provided workspace for around fifty individuals at different times.

Designed and constructed by Graham, a master craftsman, the studio was compact and well organised. Distinguished by its high quality facilities and finishes, it provided remarkable versatility within a relatively small space. A key feature of the studio was that work-spaces could be transformed into a gallery for the group's regular

open day exhibitions. Great attention was paid to detail. Lighting was activated by movement sensors, for example, in order to keep electricity costs down, and keep light switches clay free. Cleaning was facilitated by appropriate flooring surfaces, and by extensive use of trolleys for equipment and materials. Cleaning was carried out twice a week by one or two members in return for reduced rent. We subscribed to magazines communally, and successfully made joint applications for various grants. When we held joint selling exhibitions we adopted a system whereby a small percentage of each sale was placed in a group kitty, dedicated to future activities. Thus the person who sold the most work in financial terms contributed the most back.

Being part of a communal

studio offered many advantages. We often passed projects and clients on to each other, and working in close proximity prompted people to discuss their work and share information. Regular open days were arranged for the public and local schools, and we had visits from universities and international museums. Pooling resources for the open days proved particularly successful, as our combined manpower and joint financial input enabled us to stage well organised events, which generated sales direct to the public and often bought further work through the year.

As a starting point for my career, I feel that sharing ups and downs in a communal studio, and tapping into the momentum of joint motivation, was of tremendous benefit. I would certainly recommend it as a way forward for anyone who feels daunted by the financial risks or isolation of setting up a studio on their own. During the time the studio operated in this way, I greatly enjoyed the benefits of sharing, not just equipment, but also energy, problems, projects and mutual interests. However, after some years of running Balls Pond Studio I needed more workspace, and as a result we decided to draw the communal studio to a close. Recently Graham converted the building into a live-work space, and we now live on the top floor above the studio. In December 2001 we bought a house in the south of France where we are now developing a second base.

Exhibiting, selling and organising

I enjoy being organised, my style of organisation is quite chaotic. I take pleasure in providing information about my work, making proposals and all the extraneous activities involved in running a studio. The worst aspect of being self-employed is the accounting and tax work. My advice is, work out a simple method of record-keeping with your accountant when you set up in business (no matter how small), and then keep on top of it.

It takes as much time to sell a pot as it does to make one. In any one week I spend about half my working time doing things other than actually making. I used to panic that these other activities were so time consuming, and I thought that the proportion of hands-on work to organising work would improve as I became more established. This is not the case. The nature of the organising work has changed, but not reduced.

It has always been my ambition to make a living from my work, and I realised early on that it was important to learn about the business-related aspects of my profession. I paid careful attention to the business studies lessons during my seven years at college, and as soon as I finished my MA I enlisted on an eight-week business course. As a student you have to actively seek to learn, rather than submit to being passively taught. Motivation comes from within. So what advice would I offer to budding studio ceramists?

Presentation

Be organised. Communicate your image with clarity and care. You do not have to present yourself in an expensive, slick way. Your job incorporates good design, manual skills and attention to detail, so let the way you promote yourself reflect this. Materials can be simple and inexpensive, yet still be effective.

Photography

I have always tried to keep a good photographic record of my work. Even when money and time were short, I still made sure that photographs were taken. A photograph is the only record once a piece is sold. Good quality photography is essential for communicating to galleries and collectors, and for promotional purposes, for teaching and for your own archive. If your work is good but the photograph is poor, there is no point showing the photograph. Better to have one outstanding photograph than twenty mediocre ones.

Photographs are a really important tool, but they are very expensive. If money is short, find an interested photographer and ask for him/her to carry out work as an exchange or swap. Assess the purpose of the image before briefing the photographer.

Does it need to be informative or imaginative? Photographs accompanying applications for exhibitions or grants have very different requirements to a publicity shot. Perhaps you need to get the same piece photographed in several ways.

Perseverance

For every successful project, working relationship or sale, there are normally at least nine others that do not come through. Don't be put off by lack of response or rejection. If the public do not come to you, you must go to them. When we held open days at Balls Pond Studio, we would hand deliver invitations throughout the neighbourhood a week before the event. If you have a dream project that you want to achieve, get out there and tell people about it. I wanted to have a solo show two years after leaving college, but of course no galleries were making any sign of inviting me. This prompted me to stage my own exhibition by renting The Orangery in London's Holland Park in 1988. I budgeted £800, but it actually cost twice as much. I spent as much time and effort promoting and staging the show as I did making the work. Fortunately the exhibition sold well. Over the next five years I organised two further show at The Orangery. Each time I ran round the streets near the park pushing invitations through letterboxes. After the first show I understood why galleries take a cut of 50% or more of the selling price of a pot. Mounting and promoting exhibitions is an art in itself.

Perspective

Have aims and objectives clear in your mind, and make regular checks on your progress in achieving them. It could be something quite small, such as acquiring a piece of equipment, or it could be something major, a long-term ambition.

I normally take a good long break each year from the studio, spending six to eight weeks travelling. This has proved invaluable, and I regard it as a key element of my annual programme, not to mention a rest. I have a huge appetite for work, but I could not maintain the same pace physically or mentally for a full year. From the other side of the world I can view the past year's activities with detachment. Travelling also provides vital cultural and creative stimulus; it is both inspirational and educational.

It is important to be open to new influences. The rush and pressure of daily work can inhibit your creativity. You need to look at projects or situations from several angles. Keep an open mind about future directions. Don't compromise your ideals, aims and objectives, but at the same time don't be too fixed in your views.

Coda

For me, the word craft is extremely important. Craft skills are paramount to my work and I get immense pleasure from using and developing them. When I visit galleries or read about contemporary ceramics, I marvel at the high quality of work being produced around the world. The spirit in these pieces provides a reassuring reminder that we have developed a sensitive and refined culture.

Kate and her partner Graham Inglefield on the balcony of Balls Pond Studio. Security gates and balcony symbolising earth, air, fire and water made by Steven Forster. Building designed by Steve Bowkett.

FRIED ANT'S EGGS FOR STARTERS!

(Yum yum - they were good but at the end I noticed the legs!!!)

Tuesday was spent a bit hung over from the party - we went to the fabulous Archaeology Museum + then out for English Roast Beef!!!. I bought some beautiful tin Christmas tree decorations in a market + we bought a brass Rabbit for christina - we cant work out if its $40 or $400!!!.!!!!. Wednesday we went to Ixtawatanecho monastery which is now a museum - we had lunch, as usual the food was superb - we had ANTS EGGS for our starter!!!!

22 April 90.

It is now Sunday morning. Big G is snoring. Hotel Principal, Oaxaca. We have left the nest of the fantastic Gil + Christina and are alone for a few weeks to see South of Mexico. Its just like the usual trips - a nine hour coach ride through

(last Friday) 2011

beautiful scenery, winding roads and a snow capped volcano in the distance. Its a Colonial hotel with lovely courtyard. Sat. visited Monte Alban ruins on mountain top above the nestling Oaxaca - given a tour by a very inter--igent old guide who was drunk! He said that there is a period of time when Jesus went missing - 20 years and says he was here at the first university and hospital of the world!!!

We bought two beautiful tin blue moon ...... tin little wooden animals + a little

Forced to Disco DANCE IN the street!!!

dressed in veil of fertility + turban.

(free.........)

Graham on the head table

given dinner + hospitality unforgettable.

Friday 23rd Our Anniversary 4th

NOT ROUND WALKING

PATTING POTS INTO

SHAPE, FAST COILING

→ drawing with her finger in white clay.

at Ratchaburi Giant water containers being made (very fast) 26th.

carrying wet soft pots in rope slings

I stood inside the massive tunnel kiln while it was still warm from a firing. It's walls were lined with thick bubbly glaze. Raw pots were being moved around by rolling them along a human chain on their bottom rims. A hive of activity......

27th Our plans for our last week of holidays are thwarted with lack of flights — No Rangoon Mandalay or trip down the Irawaddy this time. What to do stuck in steamy city? We decided to be extrava-gant + fly to Phuket that afternoon. Fate, led us to the Marina Diving Club + onto a boat same night at 11PM heading for 4 days of snorcheling on the Similian Islands in the Andaman Sea!!!! Instead of racing round Rangoon in Burma we are on a boat at dawn of the 28th next to a tree clad empty island with hopefully turtles + lobsters around to snorchel at, A happy point to end on.

water buffalo wallow by the Lang river 21st Jan. We are in Paradise with only 24 hours to spare!! Staying in tiny bamboo hut on stilts @ 10 km from Soppong. We got here by early morning bus along high up clifts on an unfinished road. It was hair-raising.

The river runs through Tham lot caves right by our hut, we had a 3 hour tour into their beautiful caverns

at sunset we watched the birds flock into the cave-thousands upon thousands and the bats flew out.

Tham Lot Caves

a 3 hour tour by a guide with 2 wives who don't know about each other

the birds flew in + the bats flew out

we climbed big steep ladders

BOAT COFFIN CAVE

carrying lanterns wading through the river in the dark

from Guddes of draynell the most dangerous trip I have ever had!! EVER

Wed 18th April 1990

Sunday we are at last in a strange new place with people speaking a foreign language !!! Hil + Christina are the most perfect hosts - driving us from place to place + feeding us so brilliantly !!! Sunday we went with the whole family on a boat around an area of canals — HUNDREDS of boats full of flowers, brilliant fun, boats of Mariachis + with a straw + papier mache name plate with a woman's name. The whole of Mexico city used to be canals. Then Monday 1pm we started drinking — first Cuba Libras on the whole of the city then onto Pardinos seafood + singing with live Mariachis + mucho fun with then back to the house....... phew great fun......

Mexico

vessels being punted into each other, each boat woman's name, familys on picnics, ladies in little boats full of flowers, brilliant fun, boats of Mariachis + floating glokinspeils playing Mexican tunes. Then on Monday we went to Palacio Nacional + saw the Diego Rivera murals WOW !!! - staggering, brilliant, breathtaking...... + then the cathedral, which was very grand but made us angry as it was made with the stones + blood of the Aztecs! the 41st floor of a building overlooking restaurant for food, mucho Tequila, mucho dancing Raymundo, Gil, Christina, Gustavo + estola....

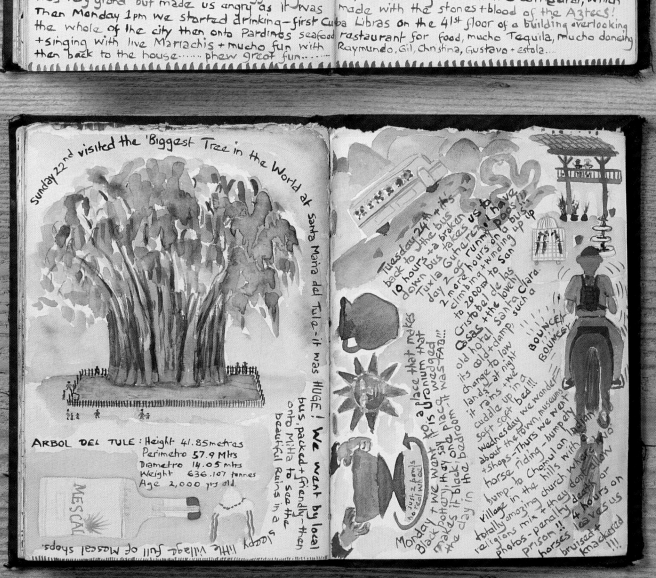

Sunday 22nd visited the 'Biggest Tree in the World at Santa Maria del Tule - it was HUGE ! We went by local bus, packed + friendly - then onto Mitla to see the beautiful Ruins in a sleepy little village full of Mescal shops.

ARBOL DEL TULE: Height 41.85 metres
Perimetro 57.9 Mtrs
Diametro 14.05 mts
Weight 636.107 tonnes
Age 2,000 yrs old

MESCAL

Just 2 bowls no real wheel

Monday + we went to a place that makes Black pottery they say that place makes it black, one day - it was FAB!!! the day in the bedroom....

Tuesday 24th + its back to the bus. The bus 10 hours + a broken down bus takes us to Tuxla Gutierrez I have day 2 of runny poos!!! 2 more hours on a bus climbing + winding up up to 2000m to San Cristobal de las Casas + the lovely Hotel Santa Clara old hotel with its old + damp, low lands + we change to low cuddle up in a it rains + we soft soft bed !!! Wednesday we wander about the town, museums + shops - Thurs we went horse riding - bumpty bump - to Chamul on Indian village in the hills with two totally amazing church religions mix + they don't allow photos - penalty death or prison !! 4 hours on horses leaves us bruised + knackered !!!

BOUNCE BOUNCEY

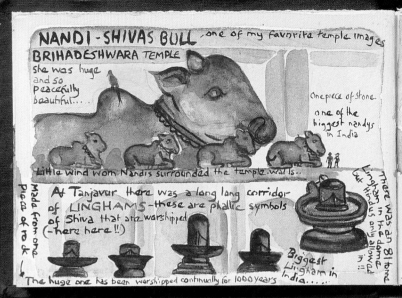

NANDI-SHIVAS BULL — one of my favorite temple images
BRIHADESHWARA TEMPLE

she was huge
and so
peacefully
beautiful....

One piece of stone.
one of the
biggest nandys
in India

Little wind worn Nandis surrounded the temple walls...

At Tanjavur there was a long long corridor of LINGHAMS—these are phallic symbols of Shiva that are worshipped (— here here !!)

There was an 8ft dome Lingham in the dome but Hindus only allowed

Made from one piece of rock

Biggest Lingham in India.....

The huge one has been worshipped continually for 1000 years

South India EATING

cooling the coffee at the table

no knives + forks

eat / with RIGHT hand. as you are supposed to clean your bum with the left.

We have taken to eating in the southern dining halls where dinner is served up on a piece of leaf + the place is a humm of activity. food is delicious..... thali, dosa, puri, pakora, lassi

a special meal costs 15 rupees (30p)

21st in the afternoon we walked down to the river and watched the elephants being scrubbed all over

it was lovely — the huge animals being so gentle lying on one side

teeth clean

they got a really thorough scrub

We watched the elephants the boys watched us !!

3. aru...

pat tap pat

So pots per day 1 rupee each

then we cycled to find a potter who was working away on his wheel his dad patting pots into final shape.... we sat for ages watching their work... Such pure craft + everything so simple

forms thrown off a lump with no base then coiled + tapped into shape...

On the 10th took a bus to visit a temple 500 steps up on a hill — the view was brilliant a panorama of paddy fields + the plains + town with big goporams below — at the temple a crazy lady tried to take our shoes because inside temples you do leave shoes - chapels theyre called — with a chapel minder..........so 11th a flight back to Goa ready to meet the Coles family from Lanzarotte... 13th picked them up at the airport + took them tired + bleary eyed from their long journey to Fatima's house + then for a swim — we all have bikes + spend days going back + forth to + along the beach playing with baby crabs + swimming... it is a treat to see the Coles but are itching also to get back on the move... Coles moved to a 5 star resort down the road. Diana has a bad cold, big G is reading loads + I enjoy playing with the girls.... we have booked 2 suites in Therrakol Fort for Sat Sun, where we stayed last year... we return in convoy of car + scooter + its as good as we remember it to be

crazy dancing using movements of the eyes eyebrows, eye muscles lips fingers + hands

Putting on the coconut oil make up

31st Jan

Faces = green = good red = bad yellow = lady

KATHA KALI THEATRE

"ART IS LARGER THAN LIFE"

Director Devan explained all!!!

Raining on the 7th

beep parp honk beep beep

I gave a slide show at Andhra university + other art staff cooked us a lovely lunch then over night AC sleeper to the packed packed of crazy calcutta HUGE noisey + full of people HOW do they all survive?! It really is teeming + bursting at it's seams - its a shock such a contrast to Ooty just last week!!!

CRAZY MONSTER OF A PACKED TO THE LIMITS CITY

We walk the streets + take in the city life.

Calcutta = crazy = crazy city CRAZY

6+7th Feb "Beep" Beep 15 MILLION PEOPLE"

as the trains pull into the stations we sit and look out of the window. The stations seems to be more busy + a real hub of activity - shops, stalls, cows, porters, families, begging children + old + young, or sometimes a small sleepy station with a few people sitting around...

It seems too late at the stations than the train is moving...

"CHAI CHAI"

Ticking by... just 7 days + the hols will be over + time is ticking by so its strange to believe I've will be in London in a week...

waiting on the station platform

Benares

The Goddess Saraswati is paraded through the streets + put onto a boat + taken into the middle of the Ganges. + SUNK!!! Dozens of times by groups of devout lads (what else is there to do for them?!)

light + generators carried

MUSIC LIGHTS + MEN GOING TRANCE CRAZY

Ganges bathers

People pilgrim to Benaries to bathe. Tiny narrow winding streets... busy busy

So we are at the Ganges, an overnight AC (unfortunately) from Calcutta landed us at Varanassi with a crowd of horrid Indian Tourist seeking commission getting the sleepy man... quite a shock from South, though we soon found Surya hotel, average room lovely garden. We took a cycle rickshaw into town + were immediatly plunged into Ganges magic.... WOW what an incredible city - the religous centre of India - you can feel it in the air

Here is a govt run Ganga shop - so I think everyone is stoned here - not us!!!

our row boat man at dawn

click click

tourists on a boat

nose of an elephant
mouth of a crocodile
eye of a monkey
ear of a pig
legs of a lion
body of a fish
tail of a peacock
this   stands over
the entrance of the
Buddhist temples, the
pattern was on the
ceiling of the cave temple
of the infinate Buddah. at
Dambulla ... high up under a huge rock !!!!!

10th Feb. Tangalla : by the sea; we sit on a platform over a lagoon + again mo33ies abound!!!

Barbed wire at Marias

room at andpas

JOHNNY HAS GONE BACK TO KUWAIT

No rooms to be found ANYWERE on North Goa coast

No JOHN + JOAN

NIGHT PARK PLAZA HOTEL + HOT SHOWERS

forced Back to Panajim

on and on +
on and on home
on

to wash in the sea

HOME HORAY

Ceremony of "our lady" of Tiger Prawn Supper

New Years Eve

very tired + early to bed ......

Bad news 17Jan - We are at WAR with Iraq...

ching me try to paint a cow —

Jan 19th sitting waiting for a bus, lots of people watching me try to paint a cow + im a bit cramped !!!! but the cow has gone away + im a bit cramped !!!! This morning we went to a beautiful bird sanctuary + then left Mysor on a 3 hour bus ride to the hills ... we are on the move again Jan 21...: no we aern't! we have stopped here at Mudumalai nature reserve to enjoy 3 nights + 2 days in the jungle - staying in Abhayaranayam sanctuary annexe - it is beautiful - elephants are scrubbed clean in the river while monkeys, woodpeckers + kingfishers + us look on - it is cooler in the hills + ve quiet...

Niligiri Hills, South India 1995

202

Kate Malone
Curriculum Vitae

Born London 1959

Training
1979-82 BA in Ceramics, Bristol Polytechnic
1983-86 MA in Ceramics, Royal College of Art, London

Solo Exhibitions
1988 *Fruits de Mer* - The Orangery, Holland Park, London
1989 *Deep Sea* - House and Garden, Nassau, Bahamas
1990 *Fruits of the Sea II* - The Orangery, Holland Park, London
         Solo Exhibition – Aberystwyth Arts Centre, Aberystwyth, Wales
1992 Solo Exhibition - Osiris Gallery, Brussels, Belgium
1993 *Fruits of the Earth* - The Orangery, Holland Park, London
1994 *Fruits of the Earth and Sea: Ceramics by Kate Malone* - Manchester City Art Galleries, Manchester
1995 *Kate Malone: New Ceramics* - The Scottish Gallery, Edinburgh
         Kate Malone Ceramics – Vincent Gallery, Exeter
1997 *Fruits of the Imagination* - Dover Street Gallery, London
1998 *The Allotment* - Midlands Arts Centre, Birmingham, followed by national tour to eleven venues from 1998-2000
2000 *Nuts and Berries* - Dover Street Gallery, London

Selected Group Exhibitions and Fairs
1987 Royal College of Art Retrospective - Kyoto, Japan
1988 Munich Art Fair - Munich, Germany
         Sotheby's Decorative Arts Exhibition – Sotheby's, London
         Out of Clay - Works in Clay by Artists, Potters and Sculptors - Manchester City Art Galleries, Manchester
1989 British Craft - Ceramic Studio, Vienna, Austria
         British Ceramics - Toronto, Canada
1992 *The Furnished Landscape* - Crafts Council, London
         Balls Pond Studio Summer Exhibition - The Economist Building, London
1993 *Crystalline Ceramics: Experiments with Glazes by 20th Century Potters* - Manchester City Art Galleries, Manchester
         The High Table - Craftspace Touring Exhibition, UK
1994 *A New Century in Design* – Tokyo Metropolitan Teien Art Museum, and Japanese Tour
         International Ceramics Fair - Adrian Sassoon, Park Lane Hotel, London
1995 *Out of this World* - Crafts Council, London
         British Contemporary Ceramics and Glass - New York, USA
         International Ceramics Fair - Adrian Sassoon, Park Lane Hotel, London
1996 SOFA, Chicago - Adrian Sassoon, Chicago, USA
         Living at Belsay - Belsay Hall, Northern Arts / English Heritage, Northumberland
1997 ART 97 - Adrian Sassoon, Business Design Centre, London
         Miami Arts Fair – Adrian Sassoon, Miami, USA
         International Ceramics Fair - Adrian Sassoon, Park Lane Hotel, London
         Animal, Vegetable, Mineral - Drumcroon Art Education Centre, Wigan
         Time For Tea - The British Council, International Touring Exhibition
1998 ART 98 - Adrian Sassoon, Business Design Centre, London
         Spirit of the Times - The Bowes Museum, Barnard Castle, County Durham
         International Ceramics Fair - Adrian Sassoon, Park Lane Hotel, London
         Fine Art and Antiques Fair - Adrian Sassoon, Olympia, London
         Working from the Collection - Ipswich Museum, Ipswich, Suffolk

1999	ART 99 - Adrian Sassoon, Business Design Centre, London
	International 20th Century Arts Fair - Adrian Sassoon, New York
	International Ceramics Fair - Adrian Sassoon, Park Lane Hotel, London
	Fine Art and Antiques Fair - Adrian Sassoon, Olympia, London
	Westerwald Preis - Germany
2000	International 20th Century Arts Fair - Adrian Sassoon, New York
	European Ceramic Masters - Steninge Slott Palace, Sweden
	International Ceramics Fair - Adrian Sassoon, Park Lane Hotel, London
	ART 2000 - Adrian Sassoon,. Business Design Centre, London
	Dish of the Day: Contemporary British Ceramics and Glass - The British Council, International Touring Exhibition
2001	*Home Sweet Home: Contemporary British Design for the Home* – The British Council, International Touring Exhibition
	British Ceramics - Galerie Norby, Copenhagen
	International Art and Design Fair - Adrian Sassoon, New York
	British Ceramics - Mark Grainer, Philadelphia
2002	ART 2002 - Adrian Sassoon, London
	Ceramic Rooms: At Home with Kate Malone and Edmund de Waal – Geffrye Museum, London
	International Art Fair – Adrian Sassoon, Grosvenor House, London
	Art & Design Fair, 7th Regiment Armoury, NYC – Adrian Sassoon
2002-3	*The Golden Age of Ceramics – Fifty Years of Pivotal Ceramists,* Red Gallery, Southsea

Large Scale Works and Public Commissions

1987	Large wall panel – Hydrotherapy Pools, Southampton General Hospital
1989	Four wall panels – Quintessence Restaurant, London (now closed)
1990	Serving platters, dishes, water jugs, fish tank accessories - Otaru Maritimo Hotel, Japan (now closed), Architect Nigel Coates
	Wall Panels and Tabletops – La Gaulette Seafood Restaurant, London (now closed)
1991	Life Pours Forth, courtyard fountain - Homerton Hospital, Hackney, London
	Rise and Shine Magic Fish water sculptures - Lea Valley Park, Hackney Marshes, London
1992	The Leaf of Life, wall sculpture, clock and wall lights – HIV and Drug Dependency Unit, West Middlesex University Hospital, Twickenham, Middlesex
1993	Bath for Birds – Chapel Allerton Hospital, Leeds
1994	Bronze Drinking Fountain - Castle Park, Bristol
	Queen Pineapple - Manchester City Art Galleries, Manchester
1995	Bronze Herb Garden Fountain - Geffrye Museum, London
1996	Swim Fishes Swim, courtyard fountain – Children's Oncology Ward, Royal Devon and Exeter General Hospital, Exeter
1997	Four large pots for two Caribbean Cruise Liners - Commissioned by London Contemporary Arts
1998	Time For Tea, large clock - Bentalls Shopping Centre, Kingston-upon-Thames, Surrey
1999	Pineapple atop the Binks Building, Northern Quarter, Manchester
2000	Bronze Millennium Fountain - Greenwich Park, Greenwich, London
2001	Undersea Garden, children's seats and courtyard ornaments – Children's Oncology Ward, Royal Devon and Exeter General Hospital, Exeter
	Mother and Daughter Pots of Symbols - The Old Bailey Consortium, London

Public Collections

Ashmolean Museum, Oxford
Brighton Museum and Art Gallery
Bristol Museum and Art Gallery
The British Council (Chairman's Collection; Manchester and Bahamas Office Collections;
    Tea Pot Collection; Touring Collection)
Cleveland Arts Centre, Middlesborough
Crafts Council Collection, London
Geffrye Museum, London
International Museum of Folk Art, Santa Fe, New Mexico
Leeds Museums and Galleries
Los Angeles County Museum of Art, California
Manchester City Art Galleries
Musée des Beaux-Arts, Montreal
Musée National de la Céramique, Sèvres, France
Norwich Castle Museum, Norfolk
Paisley Museum and Art Gallery, Scotland
The Mint Museum of Ceramic Art, Charlotte, North Carolina
The Potteries Museum, Stoke-on-Trent, Staffordshire
The J.B. Speed Art Museum, Louisville, Kentucky
Ulster Museum, Belfast, Northern Ireland
Victoria & Albert Museum, London

Selected Articles, Reviews and Catalogues

Sarah Charles, 'Deeply Alluring', *The Observer,* 1 February 1987
Tanya Harrod, 'Kate Malone – Potter of the New Spirit', *Ceramic Review,* July / August 1987
Pamela Johnson, 'Sub-Aquatic Ceramics', *Crafts,* September / October 1988
Abigail Frost, 'Fruits de Mer' Exhibition Review, *Arts Review,* September 1989
Emmanuel Cooper, 'Kate Malone', *Ceramic Series,* no.38, Aberystwyth Art Centre, December 1989
Kate Malone, 'Fruits of the Earth', *Ceramic Review,* September / October 1993
Nicole Swengley, 'Castle Park', *Crafts,* November / December 1993
Lesley Jackson, ed., *Fruits of the Earth and Sea – Ceramics by Kate Malone,* Manchester City Art Galleries, Manchester, 1994
Pamela Johnson, 'Fruits of the Earth' Exhibition Review, *Crafts,* January / February, 1994
Paul Vincent, 'Views on Recent Shows', *Studio Pottery,* October / November 1994
Alison Goddard, 'Crystal Glaze', *New Scientist,* July 1995
Will Levi Marshall, Exhibition Review, *Ceramic Review,* July / August 1995
'Crystalline Alchemy' *Ceramic Review,* March / April 1997
Exhibition Review, *Crafts,* June / July 1997
Exhibition Review, *Crafts,* October / November 1997
MAC, *The Allotment – New Ceramics by Kate Malone,* Midland Arts Centre, Birmingham, 1998
Lesley Jackson, 'Sharp Urban Potters', *The Independent,* 13 November 1998
Lesley Jackson, 'This and that', *The Guardian,* (Space supplement), 20 November 1998
Lesley Jackson, 'The Allotment' Exhibition Review, *Crafts,* January / February 1999
'The Allotment' Exhibition Review, *Ceramic Review,* Feburary / March 1999
Anatol Orient, 'Shake, Rattle and Roll', *Ceramic Review,* November / December 1999
Red Gallery, Southsea, *The Golden Age of Ceramists – 50 Years of Pivotal Ceramists,* catalogue, May 2002
Geffrye Museum, exhibition catalogue, 'Ceramic Rooms', September 2002

Selected Bibliography

Garth Clark, *The Potters Art – A Complete History of Pottery in Britain,* Phaidon, London, 1995

Jo Connell, *The Potter's Guide to Ceramic Surfaces,* Krause Books, Iola, Wisconsin, 2002

Edmund de Waal, *Ceramic Design Sourcebook,* New Holland, London, 1999

Neil French, *The Potter's Directory of Shape and Form,* A+C Black, London, 1998

Tanya Harrod, *The Crafts in Britain in the 20th Century,* Yale University Press, New Haven, 2000

Jane Heath, *The Furnished Landscape – Applied Art in Public Places,* Bellew Publishing, London, 1992

Peter Ilsley, *Macro-Crystalline Glazes – The Challenge of Crystals,* Crowood Press, Marlborough, 1999

Jo Lauria, *Colour and Fire - Defining Moments in Studio Ceramics, 1959-2000,* Los Angeles County Museum of Art, Los Angeles, 2000

Martina Margetts, *International Crafts,* Thames and Hudson, 1991

Stephen Murfitt, *The Glaze Book,* Krause Books, Iola, Wisconsin, 2002

Charlotte Speight and John Toki, *Hands in Clay,* Mayfield Publishing, Mountain View, California, 1999

Josie Warshaw, *The Complete Practical Potter,* Lorenz Books, London, 1999

Contact Addresses

Kate Malone, Balls Pond Studio, 8b Culford Mews, London, N1 4DX (kmaloneceramics@clara.co.uk)

Principal dealer: Adrian Sassoon, 14 Rutland Gate, London SW7 1BB (www.adriansassoon.com)

Acknowledgements

Kate Malone:
I would like to thank all the private collectors whose patronage has given me the confidence and encouragement to pursue my passion to make pots. Special thanks to those in Antigua, Australia, Bangkok, the Caribbean, Colorado, Germany, Japan, London, Miami, New York and Southampton Long Island.

I would like to thank all my tutors and professors, especially Pete Eveleigh, George Rayner, Mo Jupp and David Hamilton.

I would also like to acknowledge the support I have received over the years from Adrian Sassoon, Andrew Logan, Zandra Rhodes, Edmond Di Robillant and the late Jean Muir.

Finally I would like to thank Linda Lambert at A & C Black, Lesley Jackson for all her editorial help and Katy Hepburn for designing this book.

Lesley Jackson:
Many thanks to Kate for inviting me to collaborate on this book. It has been a privilege and a pleasure.

List of Photographers:
Steven Bond 145 (top right)
Stephen Brayne 2, 3, 14, 15 (mid & lower), 17 (mid & lower), 18 (top), 41, 61, 62, 81-3, 86-91, 93, 102-3, 108, 109, 112, 114-22, 125, 130, 134-7, 141, 167, 171-88, 193-203
Peter Chatterton 32-3, 40, 42-58, 76-9, 94-5, 100-1,104-5
Gugliemo Gavin 158 (top & middle left hand side)
Gina Glover 143 (bottom), 144 (middle), 145
Matthew Hollow 59, 60, 63, 66-75, 84-5, 92, 106-7, 110, 113, 123-4, 126-7, 131-3, 138-9
Rupert Horrox 191
Kate Malone 12, 15 (top), 16, 17 (top), 149-51, 169
Bryan Nash 20, 22-31, 34-8, 39 (lower), 54 (bottom), 111
Robert Posner 9 (upper)
Karen Robinson 140
Robin Scott 9 (lower)
Steven Speller 8, 19, 96-9, 154-5, 157, 158 (close-ups), 159-61, 163-5, 206
Oscar Paisley 18, 192

Whilst I have taken every care to identify the photographers whose work appears in this book, I apologise for any omissions or mistakes (Kate Malone)

Thanks to Adrian Sassoon for his kind permission to use several of the Matthew Hollow photographs.

Page 14. Zandra Rhodes Dress photo.
© The Art of Zandra Rhodes.

Index